Derek Tangye has become famous all over the world for his series of bestsellers about his flower farm in Cornwall. The series, which began with *A Gull on the Roof*, describes a simple way of life which thousands of his readers would like to adopt themselves.

Derek and his wife left their glamorous existence in London when they discovered Minack, a deserted cottage close to the cliffs of Mounts Bay. Jeannie gave up her job as Press Relations Officer of the Savoy Hotel Group and Derek Tangye resigned from MI5. They then proceeded to carve from the wild land around the cottage the meadows which became their flower farm.

Derek Tangye's bestsellers include *Cottage on a Cliff, A Cat Affair* and *The Way to Minack*.

Also by Derek Tangye in Sphere Books:

LAMA
SOMEWHERE A CAT IS WAITING
A DONKEY IN THE MEADOW
SUN ON THE LINTEL
WHEN THE WINDS BLOW
A CAT AFFAIR
THE WAY TO MINACK
THE WINDING LANE
COTTAGE ON A CLIFF
THE AMBROSE ROCK
A CAT IN THE WINDOW
A CORNISH SUMMER
A DRAKE AT THE DOOR
A GULL ON THE ROOF

A Quiet Year

DEREK TANGYE

With line drawings by Jean Nicol Tangye

SPHERE BOOKS LIMITED

First published in Great Britain by
Michael Joseph Ltd, 1984
Copyright © Derek Tangye 1984
Published by Sphere Books Ltd, 1986
27 Wright's Lane, London W8 5SW
Reprinted 1986

Set in Times

Printed and bound in Great Britain by
Cox & Wyman Ltd, Reading

To Raleigh Trevelyan
from us both

ONE

'Valentine's Day, and the post has come. There are no Valentine cards for either of us ... but there is one for Ambrose!'

Ambrose our cat.

'Let me see it.'

It was warm in the porch where we were sitting, a sunny morning, a summer-like morning. Above us was Knocker the gull, squashing his webbed feet against the glass. Knocker who maddens us sometimes as he bangs the glass with his beak, demanding attention.

Jeannie looked at the card, though it was not a card in the sense of a shop-purchased card. It had been drawn by the sender. A large heart on one side, and on the other side two cats sitting on a wall ... one of them a coquettish lady ogling

the ♥ne f♥r me

a stern gentleman cat; and a wispy line above the lady cat led to the message: 'You are the one for me!'

'I know who inspired that,' said Jeannie, 'Lovely Boy!'

Lovely Boy was a Seal Point Siamese who lived in a Mayfair flat where he was doted upon by a very old friend, Eric Hiscock, doyen of the London book world, who had known me since my anti-cat days and had watched me change my attitude. First Monty, then Lama, then Oliver and Ambrose.

'We must frame it,' said Jeannie, 'I've never known a cat receive a Valentine before.'

'I've only received one in my life myself,' I said, 'and I never discovered who sent it.'

Jeannie was sitting opposite me, the small oblong table between us, her back to the glass side of the porch which looks out on the tiny garden. She was wearing a white Arran-style sweater of cable stitching and other complicated stitches that a friend had specially knitted for her. With her dark hair, white always suited her.

'I've had three, I think,' she said, 'I never knew who sent them either. I used to look at my boyfriends and wonder. I'm not sure that I liked having them. I felt I had been put at a disadvantage.'

'Valentines can be a joke or a secret weapon,' I said, 'I remember sending one to a girl whom I thought I loved but who didn't care for me ... and I had pleasure in thinking that at last I had aroused her interest, though anonymously.'

'Subtle of you, but not very kind.'

'It didn't do any harm.'

It was unusual for us to be idle on Valentine's Day. Normally by the end of January we were picking the first of our daffodils, a variety called Magnificence, from the meadows close to the sea; and by Valentine's Day the picking would normally have become a flood. This year a dry autumn had delayed the crop.

'Let's go for a walk,' I said, 'let's take the donkeys to the Ambrose Rock.'

'Give me five minutes.'

'I'll wait for you outside.'

I left the porch and walked the few yards up to the bridge, which is not a bridge but a small patio and a stone wall, and which, when you stand there, gives you the impression of being on the bridge of a ship. You stand and gaze across the sea of Mounts Bay to the long curving outline of the Lizard.

I often muse when standing there. Indeed it is a place where my idle mind takes control of me, where I contemplate irrationally on things past, where my interest will be suddenly aroused by some movement in the moorland on the other side of the valley, alerting me into treating it with the same importance as if it were a great event. The bridge is a soothing place to be.

On the right is a grotto surrounded by wild plum trees, and on a hot summer day we have meals there in the shade of a canopy of leaves. In a corner, standing on a slab of blue slate, is an earthenware water-purifier which was given us by my mother after her first visit to Minack. At the time we fetched our water from the stream; and one day when I took my mother a morning cup of tea she found a tadpole in it. On her return to London she hurried to Harrods, and in due course the water-purifier arrived; and so the tadpoles were sieved, then returned to the stream. Later we had a well from which to draw our water, the purifier was no longer needed so it became a garden ornament.

Somewhere within the soil of the grotto, or in its neighbourhood, lies a brooch Jeannie lost two or three years after we came to Minack. Jeannie is sure it is there, obstinately sure, but a metal detector has yet to find it. She insists that she lost it after going up to fetch coal, which was stored there in those days, but though we searched and searched for it at the time, it was never found. Yet she still remains adamant that one day we will find it.

The brooch had been given to her by Gertrude Lawrence, a gold bar brooch about one and half inches long, set with small turquoise stones and with a little gold chain. At the time that Gertie gave it to Jeannie she was starring in Daphne du Maurier's play *September Tide*. She said that the little gold chain ought to have a turquoise stone in the shape of a heart fastened to it. 'Get Derek to find you one,' she added. And I did.

On the left of the bridge is the escallonia, its shiny dark-green leaves withstand the salt that sweeps in from the sea; and little pink flowers that bees love. Unfortunately the donkeys, Fred and shaggy chocolate-coloured Merlin, love the escallonia too. They snatch at the leaves as they pass

4

down the path from the donkey meadow to the stable meadow; and I curse them, especially this particular year since I had thinned out the branches and fresh young shoots were growing. It was, however, largely my fault that they were doing so or, more accurately, Fred was doing so. Merlin, successor to Penny, I kept on a halter. Fred, on the other hand as senior donkey, I allowed to be loose. Hence I was able to pull Merlin away from the fresh green shoots while Fred received my curses and a slap on his bottom.

Below the bridge is a small grassy slope and on the left of this slope, a flower bed between it and the path leading down to the stable meadow, grows Annie's Folly. It was on this slope that Penny was tethered on her first night at Minack, Penny, the black donkey, mother of Fred, whom we had bought at the end of a night out at a pub called the Plume of Feathers at Scorrier near Redruth.

Annie's Folly is in the form of a *cupressus macrocarpa*; and we call it Annie's Folly after the name of the lady who gave it to us. We had visited this lady and her spacious gardens where all manner of shrubs and heathers were grown in order to obtain a heather, a sweet-scented heather called *erica mediterranea*. The lady had pottered about her spacious garden until in a bed filled with other ericas she pounced on a small feathery-leaved plant, dug it up with a trowel and gave it to us. 'Here is your *erica mediterranea*,' she said, 'and remember when you plant it that it will grow to about four feet high.'

We planted it where Penny had been tethered; and we watched it settle down, scarcely move in growth for a year, then gradually begin to burgeon. After two years it was two feet high; after four years it was four feet high; and then, to our disquiet, it continued to grow.

'Something funny about this erica,' I said to Jeannie one summer, 'it doesn't seem to look like a heather. A heather spreads, this heather is growing upwards.'

5

And growing upwards is what it has continued to do. Hence the name of Annie's Folly. The lady, pottering in her spacious garden, had not given us an *erica mediterranea*. She had given us a *cupressus macrocarpa*; and a *cupressus macrocarpa* is a conifer which has been known to grow to a height of one hundred feet. Shall we cut it down? is the question we are often asking each other. Or do we leave it to grow taller and taller, wider and wider, increasingly obscuring the view from the bridge of the other side of the valley? I do not like to cut down living trees and so Annie's Folly is likely to stay. It is one of those problems that you leave to solve itself; and in the case of Annie's Folly it may solve itself because it is planted on a slope. A ferocious Cornish gale, the experts say, can often topple a *cupressus macrocarpa* if it is planted on a slope.

Every summer there have always been dents in the grasses in the neighbourhood of the bridge. Monty, in his day, did not have the chance to curl up close to the bridge because we had not then created it, and the only memory I have of him in the vicinity was during the first week after he had travelled with us to Minack from London. It was an occasion that I have always regretted because Monty, just outside the cottage, came face to face with a local; and the local was a tabby cat, a tabby cat who had lost a paw, obviously in a trap. I will regret always that we did not ask that tabby cat to share Minack with Monty, though I doubt that Monty would ever have agreed. Monty was not a sociable cat. In the years he was at Minack he hissed off many a caller.

Lama, therefore, was the first to make a dent in the grass close to the bridge, Lama the little black cat who came to our door in a storm, a few months after Monty had died. Lama had a special love for me and she used to curl on my lap as I sat at my desk, or choose to curl on the notepaper I was wanting to write on. She was adept at displaying the

6

power that a cat can have over a human.

On one occasion she performed a very special act for my benefit, an extraordinary act.

We had a small hut at the bottom of our cliff in which we stored the tools we used when working our cliff meadows, some of which were potato meadows, some daffodil meadows. I also used the hut occasionally to read or write in; and one summer day I was sitting there when suddenly Lama appeared with a mouse in her mouth which she dropped at my feet.

The hut was five minutes from the cottage, down a narrow path, down a number of steps, and was hidden in a copse of elder bushes. How did Lama know I was there? Why did she take such trouble to take the mouse to me? One smiles, of course, at the thought of such a well-intentioned gesture. I also marvel ... because it so happened that Jeannie saw Lama catch the mouse in the patch of ground in front of the stable, and saw her set off towards the cliff with the mouse in her mouth.

Lama was disturbed in the last year of her life by the hovering presence of Oliver, a black cat like herself. We saw Oliver for the first time from the bridge when he was hunting in the field across the valley called the clover field, on the land we now call Oliver land. Then we began to see him down the lane by Monty's Leap; and there would be times when Lama would be on the cottage side of the Leap, Oliver on the other side, resembling bookends.

He hovered around us for a year, often being shouted at by me because I was wanting to protect Lama; and then one October morning Oliver played his trump card. I was standing by Monty's Leap, Oliver in the lane a few yards away, when there was a cry from the undergrowth and out of it came a tiny ginger kitten, the double of Monty, looking exactly like Monty when I first saw him playing with a typewriter ribbon in Room 205 at the Savoy Hotel,

Jeannie's office when she was press officer of the Savoy Hotel Group.

I wrote in my diary that evening: 'I saw this ginger kitten and said to Jeannie, with all the vehemence I could command, that we must see him off . . . and she was not to feed him.' It was my inherent anti-cat attitude resurfacing.

Of course Jeannie *did* feed him, bread and milk in a saucer placed in the lane near the undergrowth to which he had soon retreated. She did this without my knowing, and I would have been angry if I had seen her doing it. But next day my attitude changed. A wooden seedbox had been left in the so-called garage and when I passed by it that morning before breakfast, a tiny ginger kitten lay curled in it. Oliver must have carried the kitten across Monty's Leap and up the lane.

Ambrose had come into our life.

'I'm ready!' I heard Jeannie call.

I had said that we would take the donkeys on our walk, but when I went over to the gate of the field above the cottage I saw they were on the far side, their backs to me, pushing their heads into the hedge, eating the brambles; and when I called out to them, they took no notice of me.

'The donkeys don't want to come,' I said to Jeannie when I joined her.

'They will,' she replied, 'soon after we have gone Fred will start hooting.'

'Too late. I'm going to leave them.'

There was also the question of Ambrose. He liked to walk with us when he was in the mood to do so; and so when we set off we were on the lookout for him. Sometimes we have reached Monty's Leap when there was a cry behind us; and on looking back we would see Ambrose bouncing down the lane. But not today. As we passed the Orlyt greenhouse we saw he was comfortably stretched out in the hay, the diminishing pile of winter hay for the donkeys.

'I dreamt last night I was young again,' I said inconsequently as we walked up the lane towards the gate which opened into Oliver land.

'Do you remember if you were glad?'

I sensed Jeannie was amused, as if I had made a funny joke.

'I woke up feeling uneasy.'

The day was very still and the sounds we heard belonged to stillness: the mew of a buzzard high in the sky, a magpie chattering, a sudden brief song of a robin, the throb of a fishing boat on her way to Newlyn, the sound of our feet on the lane. There was the sweet knowledge of privacy as we walked, at that hour of the morning at that time of year no one was likely to suddenly appear. There are those who shun privacy, preferring the noise and activity of the herd. Others value privacy beyond price. Privacy not of the hermit, but that of freedom from the raucous.

'Why uneasy?'

'I lived within a framework of permanence and permanence doesn't exist today. I am thinking of permanent values, permanent standards. One wasn't clouded as to what was right or wrong. It was simpler to control the route of one's life.'

'Do you really mean that? There was the war, and before it broke out always the shadow of war.'

'There's that shadow today. At this very moment someone could press a few buttons and every city in the country would be destroyed ... I leave war out of my reasoning. I am talking about the fabric of life as my youth knew it compared with what it is today. In the practical sense, we could walk city streets at night without fear, or go to football matches without fights breaking out around us. In the spiritual sense, we relied upon our imaginations. We read books, shut our eyes, and imagined we were living the story ourselves. We were not tempted night after night to stare at a small screen, staring thoughtlessly. We were not victims of the hype.'

We had reached the gate and I fiddled with the rope that kept it shut, untying it. We were now in Oliver land and in the field called the clover field where, from time to time, many people, young and old, look for four-leaf clovers.

'You're romancing,' said Jeannie, 'the conventional error of making the past sound more pleasant than the present.'

For a moment I was diverted by a rabbit running past in front of us, disappearing into a hole in the stone hedge on the left as we walked up the field. Too many rabbits about, I thought.

'All right, I'm romancing,' I said, 'but I didn't have to keep up with my set of friends and acquaintances by using cocaine and heroin. I could make a fool of myself by getting drunk, no harm in that except remorse. I didn't have to ruin my life as young people can do today. And if that sounds dramatic, there was something else, a simple aspect of life that is very different today. You could leave your front door unlatched with no fear of being burgled.'

'Today,' said Jeannie, and I knew she was goading me, 'there are so many schemes that are designed for young people, travel schemes, overseas voluntary work schemes, Government-sponsored work schemes and so on. You were on your own.'

True enough. I was a clerk in Unilever for a couple of years after I had left Harrow, but as I possessed no scholastic qualifications I failed to gain a coveted traineeship. I did not mind because I did not want to be chained to a large organisation; and my failure kept me free. My ambition was to live a full life and I believed my way of doing so was to become a journalist. How was it possible for me to become one?

My means of doing so could not be achieved today. I had

a girlfriend at the time who had an admirer who knew Max Aitken, Lord Beaverbrook's son, and I persuaded my girlfriend to persuade her admirer to persuade Max Aitken to give me an interview. As a result I was given a month's trial on the *Daily Express* in Manchester. That month, and the eighteen months which followed before I joined a newspaper in London, awakened me.

'You too were on your own,' I said.

Jeannie would have gone to university had she not failed her mathematics paper. She had high marks in all her other subjects, but mathematics defeated her. She would have gone to university and qualified as a schoolteacher – and we would never have met, and we would not have been walking together that morning on Oliver land.

Instead, she was to become a secretary in the Press Office at the Savoy Hotel, chosen out of thirty applicants, because she was fascinated by newspapers, and when she was interviewed was able to reel off the names of editors, and columnists, and all sorts of show people who frequented the Savoy. It was her enthusiasm, therefore, that tilted the job in her favour, that display of enthusiasm which is the passport to many a job. It was to lead to her book *Meet Me At The Savoy* and to her three hotel novels.

We had now reached the top of the field and had turned right along a track hemmed in on either side by spiky blackthorn bushes; and a hundred yards farther on we entered an area of flat scrubland spattered by the yellow of winter gorse. It was here that some badgers had a sett, flattened grass tracks leading to an elder tree where there was a cavern of a hole delving into the mud-trodden earth. It was here too that we could look back across the valley to the cottage and to our daffodil meadows falling like green stepping stones down to the sea.

We were nearing the Ambrose Rock.

'Both of us have had the luck,' said Jeannie suddenly,

'nothing worthwhile can be achieved without luck.'

'Like that afternoon when Margaret brought the jug you had ordered. Supposing you hadn't ordered it? Supposing she had postponed bringing it for a day or two?'

Margaret and her husband George are highly talented potters who live in a cottage at the end of our lane close to the main road. She is a key helper during the daffodil season, and if we have to go away for a day or two she sees that Ambrose has his fish morning and evening and that the donkeys are cared for. That particular afternoon when she brought the jug Jeannie had ordered, she broke the news that the land opposite Minack, the land on which we were now walking, was for sale. Moreover she told us that a potential buyer had already applied to the local council for permission to place a caravan within fifty yards of Monty's Leap and to establish a cesspit beside it. There were other potential buyers in the offing, she added.

Our first reaction was bewilderment. Why had no one told us about this before? Why had the farmer selling the land, who was a friend of long standing, not mentioned the sale to us? We saw him often. Our second reaction was close to panic. This land we looked out on from the cottage had been ours in our minds ever since we first came to Minack. Part of it had been used for growing early potatoes, part for daffodils, but the greater part had always been land of gorse and bracken which stretched right down to the sea's edge. It included also Carn Barges, the point overlooking Mounts Bay where Jeannie and I, after clambering up the steep slope from Lamorna, first saw Minack cottage. We had always longed to own this land and so make it safe from developers of any kind. Hence our panic.

Our bewilderment, we soon found, was the result of a misunderstanding. I called on our farmer friend and he told me he had put an advertisement in the local paper three months before, announcing that the land was for sale, and he had taken for granted that we had seen it. As we had made no approach to him, he concluded we were not interested in buying it. Then he added significantly: 'And you haven't recently been leaving any bones for Meg.' Meg was a brown and white spaniel and when we had a lamb bone we always gave it her. 'You know why?' I replied, 'we've been having topside, not lamb!'

We were now in the position of everyone else whose long-accustomed environment is threatened with destruction, but we were lucky in that we now knew the seller was sympathetic to us. We had to negotiate speedily, and again we were lucky: our bank manager was ready to help; we had a skilful solicitor; and at a crucial moment in the negotiations we were visited by an accountant friend.

We had just been told that we could have the land, all eighteen acres, at a certain price and we had decided, thinking that this would be a good business move, to make an offer below that certain price.

'Make an offer?' said my accountant friend after listening to my outline of the situation, 'make an offer? Try to save a few hundred pounds? Crazy ... it will start an auction and your rivals will put the price way out of your range. Go off and accept the price being asked.'

Then he paused.

'Here ...' he was fumbling in his pocket, 'here's 10p, go straightaway and telephone and accept!'

Thus it was that Jeannie and I became the owners of a wild untouched corner of Cornwall.

We had now reached the Ambrose Rock. It is a massive slab of granite, aeons old, and we call it the Ambrose Rock because on the first morning we took possession of the land Ambrose chose to come with us on a tour of inspection. When we reached this massive slab of granite he jumped up on it and burst into a profusion of purrs. There have been many such profusions since then: on March days when the

13

adjacent curved meadow is yellow with daffodils; on May days when bluebells touch the air with their soft scent; on summer days when foxgloves peer into the sky; and on winter days when the bracken is brown and flattened. The Ambrose Rock has become a talisman for us. Indeed we sometimes treat it as if it was a wishing-well. We touch it and wish, as if we believe there is a link between ourselves and the timeless watchfulness of the rock which gives it a secret power.

Jeannie, however, has always been in the habit of making wishes. When there is a new moon, for instance, a sliver of light in the night sky, she will perform strange antics, bowing three times to the new moon, turning round three times, blowing a kiss three times, each time secretly making her wish.

I also play the wishing game but I do not always keep my wishes secret. On this occasion when we reached the rock I touched it and made a wish. Then Jeannie asked me what wish I had made.

'I wish for a quiet year,' I replied, rubbing the palm of my hand against the rough granite.

TWO

'I'm taking a basket down the cliff,' I said to Jeannie next morning after breakfast, 'to see how the daffodils are moving.'

'I'll come with you.'

We call it the cliff, though of course it is not a proper cliff. It is land which steeply slopes to the rocks and the sea, a land of small meadows in unorganised shapes. When we first came to Minack there were such meadows all along the coast of Mounts Bay, meadows of early potatoes or early daffodils, prosperous meadows, meadows that were envied by those who did not have any. So when we left London to make our home at Minack, Jeannie and I were confident that if we carved meadows of our own out of the undergrowth we rented, we would be able to earn enough to survive.

These meadows to which we were going, therefore, were our personal meadows. Every corner of them we knew. Every badger path which ran through them. Every half submerged rock. We had created them. We had slashed the undergrowth, turned the ground, and over the years we had worked them, digging potatoes on hot summer days, picking daffodils when elsewhere the country was covered with snow. They had also been part of our weakness, our refusal to move with the times.

When we began, amateurs could earn a living from a flower farm in the area where we lived. True, there was the occasional devastation by gales, very occasionally by frost, but for most of the time the climate was on our side. Winters were warm and violets, anemones, calendula, flourished in the open ground; and the daffodils were ready to be sent to market long before those up-country were even showing through the soil. Cornish growers, therefore, were on their own in marketing flowers. No competition at that time from vast greenhouse hangars of forced daffodils. No competition from prairie-sized fields of daffodils, fields kept free of weeds by chemical sprays. The flowers we grew were as nature intended them to grow.

It was a period when parish worlds were stable and the lives of villagers were governed by the seasons. A horse or two could still be seen pulling a plough, wages did not automatically rise each year, a pound spent in a pub meant a thick head in the morning, unemployment was five hundred thousand, a dark face a rarity, hedges were cut by a sickle, bracken-covered meadows by a Father-Time scythe. There was a sense of permanence, steady jobs would always be steady, values maintained, the moon was safe from Man, great industries would always be great industries. Television had not reached into every home, extolling violence, creating envy. The silicon chip was still a dream in the inventor's mind. Life was safe for those who wanted to play it safe. Opportunities awaited those who were ready to take a risk.

Nobody could repeat today what Jeannie and I were able to do. Land was cheap then, cottages were empty and landlords were happy to rent them at nominal rates. Not quite as easy as that. It took us a year after first seeing Minack to persuade the farmer responsible for the cottage and the land that we were genuine in our wish to live there, and that we were not like those holidaymakers who, after a happy sunny holiday, declare that they have found their earthly Nirvana, and then give up when the gales and the rain set in.

16

I had an advantage in that I am Cornish, that my grandfather Sir Richard Tangye was born in Broad Lane, Redruth, where his parents kept a shop and a smallholding, and whence he set off with his brothers to Birmingham and there achieved engineering immortality by launching with hydraulic jacks the stranded Great Eastern liner built by Brunel from the slipway at Millwall docks. He created the great Cornwall Works of Tangyes in Birmingham whose engineering products are still in working order in many parts of the world.

Then there was my father who was a Deputy Lieutenant of Cornwall, a non-executive post which required him to dress up in a Gilbert-and-Sullivan-type uniform (sometimes for fun he would wear it on Christmas Day, and make us all laugh). My father had an unswerving loyalty to the traditions which he believed to be the foundation of Britain's greatness. He detested the sneerers who offered no constructive alternative to society, except the lowering of its standards, and I remember his disapproval when, in the inevitable period of youthful rebellion, I was vociferous against the Government of the day (Stanley Baldwin was my chief target) and was ardent in my support of the League of Nations. But he was amused when after my first book was published, a travel book called *Time was Mine*, our local vicar denounced it from the pulpit. The vicar thought I had been too explicit.

My background, therefore, helped to persuade the farmer we were courting that we were genuine in our wish to make our home in Cornwall. Yet he had little faith that Jeannie would stay for long. 'I reckoned six months', he told me a long time afterwards, 'before she would give up.' It was incomprehensible to him that a girl whom an American magazine had described as 'the prettiest publicity girl in the world' should wish to surrender a glamorous career at the Savoy Hotel for a primitive cottage without running water or electricity and only a paraffin stove for cooking.

We could not have changed the course of our lives in that fashion had it been today. We could not have run away from what we both believed was destroying the integrity of our true selves:

'The glamour and hospitality act as a narcotic, doping the finer aspects of living, in the grey hours of early morning you lie awake painfully aware that you live in a flashy world where truth and integrity for the most part are despised, where slickness reigns supreme.' These words are as true now as when I wrote them in *A Gull on the Roof*.

We could not have escaped because the cost of doing so would have been far, far beyond our means. We had only a few hundred pounds in the bank when we left London for Minack, but the rent for the cottage and the six acres was only £25 a year and our normal expenses amounted to £3 a week.

So we were lucky in our timing. Lucky, too, because of our isolation, that there was no pressure upon us to keep up appearances. When we were broke we could hide, and sometimes we were so broke that we hadn't the money to buy a gallon of petrol. Yet Jeannie, accustomed as she had been to a life of high sophistication, whose admirers included film stars of world renown, never suggested giving up. We went on working the land and living like nineteenth-century peasants, and experiencing naïve moments of exultation when a consignment of our new potatoes or a box of our daffodils fetched a high price in the market.

I wonder, in retrospect, what motivated us. Neither of us at the time had any intention of writing about the life we were leading. Jeannie was in fact soon to write *Meet Me At The Savoy*, but she had no expectation of becoming a novelist, and now she has written three novels. (*Hotel Regina, Home is the Hotel* and *Bertioni's Hotel*). True, I had already written three books, including the travel book

Time was Mine, story of a youthful journey around the world, and a book about the British Commonwealth, one hundred and fifty thousand words long, called *One King*. Field Marshal Montgomery ordered his staff on Luneburg Heath to read it, then he would question them about it, disconcertingly as far as they were concerned, as he sat at the head of the table at breakfast. Yet I too had no expectation of writing a book. So what motivated us? It was not as if it had yet become fashionable to talk about leaving town life for the countryside. We were considered eccentrics. Crazy.

I believe one reason was that neither of us really possesses the killer instinct, the ruthlessness which drives the ambitious in their quest for power and money. I had it once, when I was beginning my journalistic career – and then I was so ruthless that I did not mind what I said or did if it was a means of getting my story. Then I began to find that success does not automatically result in happiness, and that it is thirsty, and the thirst is never satisfied. I saw this in some of the famous people I met, people who were at the height of their profession and who were struggling to stay there; and I found it in myself. Once my vanity had been satisfied, once I had achieved my youthful ambitions, the killer instinct within me died. In its place came a wish to enjoy my life.

Jeannie also, at the beginning, was ambitious, but it is difficult to believe that she was ever ruthless. She knew what she wanted but she did not set out to gain an objective by deceit. Her successes were due to her enthusiasm, intuition and flair, an indefinable combination that caused her to be loved by those who came to know her. How strange it is to think that one day, just after she had left school, she saw in Piccadilly on the top of a bus a photograph of me, a photograph advertising my daily article in a national newspaper. Jeannie will tell you how she reacted. 'Who's he?' she asked herself. 'Who's he to get such publicity?'

There were other coincidences in our lives long before we first met. Jeannie's family once rented a small house opposite the traditional wrestling ground in Tower Road, Newquay; my family also once rented the same house. The German headmistress of Jeannie's school at Westgate on Sea had a brother who had an English language school in Bonn; my brother Colin went there. Jeannie's home was at St Albans and when both she and her sister Barbara were first working in London, they always agreed to meet on the platform at St Pancras opposite the advertisement of Tangye Oil Engines. When, on my world tour, I had my hand read. I was told by the palmist that I would marry a girl with the initials J.E.; on my first dinner date with Jeannie I discovered that these were her initials.

We were, it seems, destined to be together at Minack.

I said we failed to move with the times, and yet that statement is a little unfair. At one stage we were left some money and instead of spending it on personal comforts we invested in five large greenhouses with oil-fired equipment. This investment, we argued, was an insurance for our future; and for a while they were highly productive, and we grew a variety of profitable crops like freesias during the winter and tomatoes in the summer. We did not, however, anticipate the fact that greenhouses would become fashionable and that they would sprout up in market gardens all over the country. Nor did we anticipate the fact that European flowers and produce would be ferried across the Channel in juggernaut lorries, nor that air freight would change the pattern of the markets by flying in produce from all parts of the world, nor that oil prices would leap. We plodded on, unchanging in our growing methods, believing, like the Cornish tin-miners of long ago, that science stood still.

It was now that we failed to move with the times. We were

urged to be more business-like by the well-meaning advisers from the Ministry of Agriculture's Advisory Service. And more business-like meant that we should combat the falling prices by investing in new equipment, making the greenhouses as automatic as a factory unit for instance. And in the fields where the daffodils grew in the open we should use chemical sprays to control the weed growth; and we should install bulb-sterilising equipment, and a bulb-grading unit so that we would be able to take advantage of a developing export of Cornish daffodil bulbs.

However, we were so lacking in initiative, so content in our peasant way of life, that we refused to entertain such prospects of business efficiency; and if at the time we may have been criticised for our attitude, the future proved how correct we had been in making this decision. For we would have been saddled with the repayment of the loan that our expansion would have required; and, because horticulture depends inevitably on an excessive amount of hand labour, our wages bill would have become astronomical. At the time we had two girls and a man working regularly for us and the total wages were in the region of £1,200 a year. The wages of the three today would be in the region of £12,000 a year, yet the prices we receive in the market for daffodils have substantially dropped.

The two girls, Shelagh and Jane, and Geoffrey, were special. Shelagh was illegitimate and her foster mother came to live in the district when Shelagh was just reaching her teens. It so happened that Shelagh's real mother, unknown to Shelagh, also lived in the district, and one day Shelagh, who ran errands for the then local shop and post office, was despatched to a house with a telegram. On her return she was asked by someone in the post office as to who had accepted the telegram, and Shelagh described the woman who had done so. 'That,' said the person who had asked the question, 'was your real mother.'

Shelagh, pretty, fey Shelagh, was one of those who had doom written on her birth certificate. I remember the first time she came down the winding lane asking for a job and we had to tell her that we had just taken on another girl, Jane; and in telling her this we both felt uncomfortable, for she looked so sad. We decided, watching her going back up the lane, that we would find a way of employing her as soon as possible. So she came to Minack in due course and performed all manner of tasks apart from working on the land. She was a skilled seamstress and one Christmas she gave us a pair of quilted satin nightclothes-cases made by herself and on which she had sewn Him and Hers.

Another time, for another Christmas, she secretly took a photograph of Lama. We still have the photograph in the same frame she gave us, Lama in her first weeks at Minack, sitting on the white seat opposite the barn. But there was always an aura of doom about Shelagh and she died, a week before her twenty-first birthday, bicycling to Minack. No one knew she had a weak heart. There had been no warning.

Geoffrey was known as the best shovel man in the district,

and this in early potato terms was a qualification as important as a university degree. We used to plant eight tons of potato seed when Geoffrey first worked for us and every seed potato was planted by hand in our sloping meadows. He would plunge his long-handle shovel into the soil and dig a foot-wide voor up the meadow, and Jeannie or I would follow dropping the seed potatoes seven inches apart. The soil of the next voor he dug covered the seed potatoes in the first. Already in the autumn he would have dug over all the meadows, so at planting time the ground was clear of weeds. Then in early May harvest-time began, and Geoffrey's long-handle shovel would prise up the potato plants, and we would gather up the little potatoes, ejaculating sometimes when they were a good size: 'These are fine samples, Geoffrey!'

He was also responsible for planting the daffodil bulbs, several tons of them, both in the steeply sloping cliff meadows and in the fields we later rented. The cliff meadows were planted by long-handle shovel, the fields by a tractor we acquired; and those bulbs he planted remain the base of our daffodil income today. Of course, we should have dug them up and sterilised them, split them, planted them again; and had we done this every three years, as the experts advised us, we would have a far greater number of daffodils to pick than today. But what would have been the cost? Good ideas have a maddening ability to disintegrate when the mind of an accountant takes charge; and in this case it was my own limited accountancy mind, and intuition, that Minack land was not fitted for conventional business efficiency. The land was too rocky and much of it too steep. If we had entered the race for efficiency, the map of the land would have made us lose.

Then there was Jane. I remember Jane coming up the path for the first time to the cottage, in jeans, fair hair falling to her shoulders, a pink shirt, bare-footed, fourteen years old; and, her words tumbling out, telling us that her mother had come to live at a farm a mile or so away to be the herdswoman for the farmer; and that they were living in one of the farm cottages overlooking the sea; and that she didn't intend to stay at school after her fifteenth birthday in two months time, and she wanted to work for Jeannie and me. Jane imposed herself upon us. We never regretted it. A month after this Valentine's Day I was to see Jane one early evening coming down the winding lane again, arriving by the barn, two plastic bags in her hands, one with plants to give us, one containing her personal belongings.

But before that evening we had experienced the turmoil of the daffodil harvest. First there had been that walk down the cliff to see how they were moving, picking a few Magnificence but not enough to send away. Then, quite suddenly, after a mild couple of days, we found a profusion of stems with tight buds which were ready to pick and send to market. Not enough to have extra help, but enough to keep Jeannie and myself very busy.

Tight bulbs, as many people know, are the fashionable way today of buying daffodils. For many reasons such buying of tight bulbs offers value for money. After all, when we began to sell daffodils the wholesale markets demanded that all blooms in a box should be wide open. The wholesalers would send a note of complaint when a bud had been included in a bunch: 'Too tight' would be scrawled on the invoice. And so growers like ourselves would force overnight the daffodils we had picked during the day by keeping them in a hut which was stifled by the heat of paraffin stoves. In the evening the day's picking in bud ... next morning in full bloom.

Obviously a daffodil in full bloom, forced by paraffin heat, had a short vase life, and so there came a time when the leaders of the flower trade, inspired by the views of the Dutch daffodil specialists, began a campaign for the marketing of daffodils in bud.

As sometimes happens with missionary-type campaigns, the campaign produced unsuspected problems both for daffodil buyers and daffodil growers. Daffodil buyers, for instance, who were of a romantic nature, looking for a bunch of yellow daffodils to give their loves, found only pencil-type stems with a bud at the top; while professional buyers, whose object was to have daffodils to decorate a function, found they had to do their own forcing by heat in order to have the daffodils in bloom in time.

The problems of the growers, as one might expect, revolved around the weather. Early in the season, with cold weather and long nights, the buds stayed buds and we were able to send them away in the condition the market desired. But when the weather changed, entered a mild spell, the nights shorter, there began the rush to pick before the buds burst. We listened anxiously to the weather forecast and when it was announced that the morrow would be sunny with temperatures above the average, we did not rejoice as others would be rejoicing. We cursed. The sun would cost us money. A meadow might have to be left unpicked for lack of time, a shimmer of yellow covering it, soon to erupt into a carpet of open daffodils which, on a stranger seeing it, would cause him to exclaim how wonderful it was to be in Cornwall at daffodil time.

This spring we were to have an additional problem. Ever since commercial daffodil growing had commenced in the Isles of Scilly at the end of the nineteenth century, the method of transporting flowers to the market had been by railway. The boxes of Scilly flowers were shipped to Penzance docks, then transported to Penzance station, and there would be great activity on the platform of the flower train, as it was called, as lorries, cars, landrovers, arrived with their loads from flower farms in the West Cornwall district.

The flower train, in due course, was cancelled by British Railways. The excitement of bunching and packing to the very last moment, the twenty-minute rush up the lane to the road, past Lamorna Turn, Sheffield, Newlyn Bridge, and along the promenade road to the harbour, past Trinity House headquarters and then the last lap to the station to be welcomed by the urgent cries of porters like George Mills, Donald and Barry: 'You've just done it! ... back up to this van ... twenty boxes, thirty? ... you've done well!' All of them part of our endeavour, enthusiastic in their work, friends, displaying involvement in the crisis time of daffodil growers. These pleasures came to an end.

British Railways had come to the conclusion that the flower train was unprofitable and if they were to carry on with the service they would have to increase the freight charges. I can understand this attitude. Flower boxes require much hand labour: apart from loading at Penzance or any other station on the daffodil route, there was the unloading at Paddington station and then reloading into lorries to carry them to New Covent Garden at distant Nine Elms, hand labour all the way. It was when the old Covent Garden was closed and Nine Elms opened that the accountants of British Railways decided to withdraw the flower train by asking for freight charges far beyond what the representatives of growers, the Society of Growers as it was called, were prepared to agree to.

Perhaps, however, one day the flower train will return. But this daffodil season we had a new regime. Instead of rushing to Penzance station we had to rush a mile further on to the juggernaut lorries of the Society of Growers at a place called Long Rock. Here were based two long-term friends of mine, Ben Green and Russ, who on behalf of this co-operative organised the distribution throughout the country of the produce of the Scillies and West Cornwall, whether it was potatoes, broccoli, spring cabbage or daffodils. Their concern, and practical advice, were invaluable – and their task a formidable one.

The juggernauts scared me. When I delivered my cardboard boxes of daffodils to the flower train, I used to worry if there were only a few boxes stacked on top of mine in the van. When I delivered them to a juggernaut lorry there was the prospect of a mountain of boxes on top of them and I would lie, at a sleepless period of the night, imagining the juggernaut charging up the M5 and M4, our boxes at the bottom of the pile, being squashed.

There were also, during this period of the new regime, the difficulties surrounding the juggernaut timetables. The flower train used to run every day of the week including Sundays. This meant that the flowers arrived fresh for the early Monday morning market. It also meant that the meadows were picked clean and we could start the following week without a backlog of unpicked blooms. The juggernaut timetables were not so amenable. For instance, the last juggernaut left Penzance at 2 pm on Thursdays, with no service at all on Fridays and Sundays. Although there was a Saturday juggernaut, the daffodils it carried were the daffodils that had been picked on Thursday afternoon and Friday. These daffodils, therefore, were not in the markets until the Monday.

Yet in many cases they would appear fresh in that the buds were still tight; and this again illustrated how Jeannie and I were not moving with the times. For the big growers installed cold rooms, large areas in an insulated shed or building where blooms are held back at inconvenient times of sending.

Thus Jeannie and I were at a disadvantage with the new regime, and especially during this particular February and March because it was more often mild than cold. Hence, when our last picking and packing of the week was loaded on the juggernaut at 2 pm on a Thursday, we were helpless. We had to watch meadows change from bud to bursting bud, from bursting bud to full bloom and accept the fact

27

that we would never be able to sell them.

Such occasions depressed us, but the depression would be swept away on Monday morning when our two helpers arrived: Margaret, the potter, and Joan, once a secretary in London. Joan was a new helper. She and her husband tired of city life and set out to make a new one in Cornwall. They arrived one day in Penzance with little money and without any prospects. She became a chambermaid while her husband looked for a job. Eventually he became a milk lorry driver while she continued to take on any work available, which was to include typing Jeannie's novel *Bertioni's Hotel*.

These two, Margaret and Joan, infected us with their enthusiasm; and their enthusiasm would be put to the test when the gales blew or the rain lashed them as they were out in a field, bent double, picking, picking, picking. Then when their baskets were full they would lug them back to the small greenhouse which we used as a packing shed and dump them on the bench, and be ready to go out again until I said they were crazy and they should stay in and bunch.

One thrives when people who are working for you are on your side, appreciating the problems, sympathising over failures, rejoicing when there is success, never grumbling. We have had times when helpers have arrived in the morning and in the instant of their arrival we knew that they intended the day to be a dirge. We would try to be bright, make jokes, fuss over them and the response would be as dreary as a foggy day. In such situations one blesses the ever-increasing wages, for a point is reached when one can no longer afford to pay them and one is suddenly free.

None the less, enthusiasm such as that of Margaret and Joan has to be fuelled – and we were to have such a fuelling from Harrods.

One of their buyers had seen in Covent Garden daffodils we had been sending called, in Cornwall, *obvallaris*, the botanical name of a daffodil first discovered growing wild in Wales at the end of the last century called Tenby. Such a lovely little daffodil, like a miniature King Alfred, and it has always surprised me that the large professional growers ignored it. Perhaps it is because it has an unreliable flowering record; a year, two years may go by and there is hardly a bloom to be seen. Then a year will come when there is a profusion.

There was a profusion this year when Harrods, through our Covent Garden wholesaler, gave an order for fifty dozen bunches towards the decoration of the main hall during a British Week. All the fashionable daffodils were available for Harrods; daffodils with high-sounding names like Golden Ducat and Unsurpassable and Golden Harvest, yet they had chosen our humble *obvallaris*.

Those who saw them in the main hall, overheated, overcrowded, a humming noise of conversation, could not be expected to imagine whence they came.

They could not imagine they had come from meadows overlooking the sea of Mounts Bay; meadows bounded by blue elvin rocks and thick hedges of blackthorn; meadows with trowel-shaped holes where a badger had been digging for a bluebell bulb; meadows where if you are picking in the early morning you catch the scent of a fox as you bend; meadows poised over a turbulent sea where a gannet might be diving unafraid; meadows so sheltered by ancient stone hedges and rock formations that you can stand there untouched by the wind or by a gale which roars at you when you leave the peace of the cliff. In such meadows we picked the *obvallaris* for Harrods ... natural daffodils of the cliffs which had been growing there for decade upon decade.

Understandable, therefore, that when we had picked them, and bunched them, and packed them, and sent them away on the juggernaut, that Jeannie, in a sentimental mood, said to me: 'I wish we had left them where they were.'

The daffodil season, as I have said, was over by the evening that Jane walked down the winding lane with her two plastic bags.

'Where are you staying?' I asked when greeting her in one of those moments when one says something without thinking first.

Jane looked at Jeannie, and didn't answer.

'Oh, of course,' I hastily added, 'you're staying here the night.'

There were times when Jane was working for us that I was trivially annoyed with her. She was an ally, for instance, of Jeannie when Lama first began to haunt our environment. I did not want Lama, I said so repeatedly. Yet I would suddenly find an empty saucer halfway down the lane, another in the grass beside the barns, and I would realise that Jeannie and Jane were feeding the cat.

Another occasion was the day of the Penzance Flower Show, a year after Jane had left us to live on Tresco in the Scilly Isles, a day that witnessed the worst storm in living memory. Jane had arrived to stay with us the night before, bringing with her a collection of daffodils from the Tresco Gardens which she planned to enter for the most prestigious cup in the show, the Prince of Wales Cup which every West Country professional grower coveted.

She chose to put her daffodils in our Orlyt greenhouse, which is a hundred feet long and twenty feet wide. But overnight this ferocious gale blew up and by the morning the long greenhouse was swaying in the gale, a terrifying sight threatening disaster at any moment. Meanwhile Jane's daffodils remained inside.

Soon after breakfast I had to drive into Penzance, but before I left I warned Jane and Jeannie that they must not go near the greenhouse, let alone open the door. I had recently read of an accident of a man being lacerated by the glass in such a gale. They did not heed me. When I returned

30

I found two smiling faces, the prize daffodils no longer in the greenhouse, and Jane packing them expertly in a carboard box. A couple of hours later the box was lying alongside other entries for the Prince of Wales Cup ... and it was chosen to be the winner. Jane was the youngest person ever to win the coveted cup.

She left Tresco to live on nearby Bryher for a while and she was married in Bryher chapel to a Yorkshireman, Dick Bird, who had come to live in the Scillies. Her gypsy nature did not suggest she would wish for a formal wedding, but she proved us wrong. Apparently she had always dreamt of a white wedding and so she came to Penzance on her own (her mother had recently died) and, with the little money she had to spare, bought a wedding dress and veil.

On her wedding day, however, she reverted to her gypsy nature. She rode to chapel arrayed in her finery on a tractor, and with her dalmatian as a bridesmaid!

Jeannie and I are now godparents to her daughter Sylvia. The family have returned to Tresco. Dick is a craftsman in wood, modelling during his spare time but, he, like Jane, is employed in the famous Tresco Gardens.

Jane is responsible for the propagation department, which produces all the hedging and windbreak material for the island; four thousand conifers and one thousand eucalyptus in the past two years; and she raises the new seed which is sent to Tresco by garden specialists from all over the world; and she also raises the bedding plants needed for the Gardens.

As I listened to her that evening, describing her work, my mind went back to that moment when I first saw her, fourteen years old, fair hair falling to her shoulders, and I thought of the mountains that can be climbed, whatever the difficulties, if one had enthusiasm and a secret faith in oneself. Jane had never received any formal training, never went to school again after she was fifteen, and now she was

31

in this position of enviable responsibility in one of the most famous gardens in the world.

'I also look after the succulent collection,' she went on, becoming more technical, 'and the *pelargonium* collection which have a lot of old Victorian hybrids ... and the most exciting job I've had to do is raising new *proteas*, very exciting because they are likely to die during the first years and so when I've got them through to planting size I feel I've achieved something very special.'

Before she went to bed she told us that she would be up very early in the morning so we were not to worry if we heard any noise.

'I want to see my meadow,' she explained.

Her meadow was close to the sea, below the cottage where she had lived when she worked for us. She had created it out of waste land. She cleared the couch grass and the brambles, and she dug the soil with a Cornish long-handle shovel, bigger than herself; and did so, after a working day, at night when the moon was full, lighting the cliff and the sea beneath.

I did not hear any noise in the morning. Jane slipped out of the cottage, then along the path to the wild cliff where jackdaws nest in their dozens, and clambered down the cliff

to her meadow, a few square feet which will always be known as Jane's meadow. A memorial to innocence.

'What did you find?' I asked on her return, after Jeannie and I had dressed and Jeannie was preparing breakfast. 'Were your daffodils still flowering?'

She had planted in her meadow three varieties of daffodils: Tunis, Flower Record and Armada.

'Oh yes,' she replied, making me feel I had asked a most unnecessary question, 'unless someone digs them up they will always be flowering.'

Permanent. Like the rocks and the sea below them.

THREE

The daffodil season was over, but the daffodils remained. Market prices had dropped when the up-country daffodils came into production, the vast prairie fields of Lincolnshire, and it was no longer economical to send them to market, and so, instead of picking, we could stand and stare and marvel at the sight of our daffodils.

They lined either side of the winding lane, Coverack Glory these daffodils were called, and their yellow heads nodded in the breeze. Others peered through brambles in the hedges, poking unscathed through the thorns. In the meadows we had picked, latecomers surprised us by their number. They turned a meadow which we had cropped from being green with leaves into a repeat mass of blooms, prompting a visitor to irritate us by remarking: 'So you have given up selling daffodils.' Old-fashioned daffodils came into their own at this period, daffodils we had long discarded because of their lack of commercial value: Princeps, Bernardino, Croesus, Campanella, Sunrise, Laurens Koster, Lucifer bloomed profoundly. And down the cliff, its background the sea, there was a meadow of dazzling yellow California which bloom, year after year, too late for the daffodil market. We found it pleasing that they should be there. They would have been in a dustbin had we picked them.

The daffodil season over, we could now return to routine work, routine pleasures; and one of these pleasures was observing Ambrose in his private world.

He enjoyed sniffing the daffodils and he would wander up the lane, pausing at one bloom or another; and although this pastoral walk was a delight to watch, I was aware that he treated it as a potential excitement. It was a promising hunting ground because at daffodil-time there were many young rabbits about, young rabbits nibbling grass that was surrounded by daffodil clumps, half hiding them; and so Ambrose was on the watch, as he sniffed a daffodil, for a capture. If however, a capture eluded him he would settle down outside a hole waiting for a foolish young rabbit to emerge; and this would produce an example of cat one-track-mindedness which can end in disaster. I am always on guard at daffodil-time, any time for that matter, when Ambrose has wandered up the lane.

A sad wonder of cat life is that cats have no road sense. So intelligent, so alert to the gentlest of noises, so able to look after their personal welfare, yet they have no awareness of speed. Every hour of the day there is somewhere a cat, a confident cat, a cat busy on some personal mission, a cat with a loving and comfortable home, who is blind to the dangers of the road.

I have heard the story too often, shared in my mind the agony of loss, and then been grateful for the warning it has given me. It is easy to become complacent about everyday living, allowing habit to dull the sense of watchfulness – a hasty run down a path resulting in a fall, a careless use of a familiar tool, unnecessary haste in a car when nearing home – and so one can be grateful if somebody else's misfortune wakes one up from complacency.

I became especially alert about Ambrose when a close friend of mine, living in similar remoteness at the end of a long lane, lost his cat when it was killed by a delivery van driving down the lane. The van had been travelling at normal speed, but the cat, overconfident in his remote surroundings, was caught unawares. Ambrose, I worried, might also be caught unawares as he sat beside the lane, one-track-minded, intent on waiting for a rabbit to appear.

Hence, when the delivery of our morning mail was changed from a girl pedalling from St Buryan on a bicycle to a little red Post Office van coming from Penzance, the driver of the van was earnestly approached by me.

'You see,' I said, apologetically, feeling guilty that I was making an unnecessary fuss about a cat, 'our cat may be on the lookout for a rabbit when you come down the lane and he might be hidden in the grass and you wouldn't see him, and out of fright he might run out in front of the van.'

The reply, expectedly, was reassuring.

'I wouldn't hurt your cat for the world, any cat. Not for the world.'

Yet reassuring as the words may have sounded, I have remained on guard; and periodically, at postal delivery time, when I did not know the whereabouts of Ambrose, I will hurry up the lane, calling him, looking into the grass at the side; and from time to time I will repeat my anxiety to the postman: 'Please look out for Ambrose.'

The lane, however, does not encourage speedy driving. It is narrow and for much of the way there is a ditch at the side which occasional car drivers have failed to notice; and a tractor has been required to pull them out. Those who visit us sometimes leave their cars at the top of the hill and walk. Those who cling to their cars must tolerate the hazards; and the hazards, besides the ditch, include two other factors. There are potholes, as one might expect, but there is also the way that wheels of cars and tractors have worn down the track so that there is a hump of grassy earth in some centre parts of the lane, so that the undercarriage of a car might scrape it.

The most risky part of the entrance to Minack is, however, Monty's Leap. All through the year, except in a dry summer, a rush of water passes across the lane, tumbling afterwards first through our small reservoir, then on a rock-strewn route to the cliff and the sea. This stream, in which blackbirds, thrushes, woodpigeons, dunnocks, robins, chaffinches, green woodpeckers, like to splash as it crosses the lane, is like a miniature valley. Periodically I fill it up with small stones, but the stream wears them away. Hence if a car crosses it too quickly it is in danger of losing its exhaust pipe. I have had this happen to my own car. We had been to London and I was so pleased at coming home that I forgot the dangers of Monty's Leap, crossed it too fast ... and that was the end of the exhaust pipe.

I sense, however, that I may have exaggerated the condition of the lane. We are content with it, but it is not a lane for speedy drivers. Nor, as it happens, is it a lane for lorries.

At the approach to Monty's Leap, for instance, there is the entrance gate; and this gate hangs on a massive upright slab of granite. One day, a few years ago, we saw a group of men around this slab, notebooks, rulers and compasses in their hands. When I asked them what they were doing they explained that they were engaged in planning the building of Tater-du Lighthouse, the lighthouse which was to be the scene of the loss of the Union Star and the Mousehole lifeboat. But what was significant about our slab of granite? They did not tell me, and I have never been able to discover its significance.

Its existence, however, causes trouble for lorries. True there was a time when lorries or delivery vans could arrive with comparative ease; but today, as lorries and delivery vans having become larger and larger over the years, it is an act of adventure for them to come down the lane. Some drivers have been amused, some have cursed. Some of them on arrival have charmed us by exclaiming: 'What a lovely place ... just look at that view!' Others, their lorries having scraped against the slab of granite, swear they never will come down again. I understand their feelings and as a result we now seldom order any goods which might be delivered by lorry. None the less, incidents continue to occur from time to time.

Recently, for instance, I was standing on the patch of ground above the cottage where we have the washing line when, way across the fields by the farm I saw a huge yellow object edging its way down the lane. It was soon obscured by the wood and so I could only listen to its progress: a clattering, a sudden revving of the engine, a menacing scraping sound as if a wheel had hit a rock.

As I walked back towards the cottage, I saw the huge yellow object make the turn by the gate of the clover field where the donkeys were standing, staring in astonishment. The object lumbered towards Monty's Leap, and the slab of granite, and the narrow entrance. I realised it would be a miracle if it passed through without leaving some of its paint behind on the slab, but there was half an inch to spare and it bumped over Monty's Leap, safe. Then it met another hazard as it snorted towards where I was now standing in front of the cottage – overhanging willow branches which clawed at its roof top. The huge yellow object was a National Carrier delivery van.

The driver glared out of the car window.

'I'm bloody well not coming down here ever again!' he shouted.

He had brought a case of wine, a present from a friend.

'Calm it,' I replied, 'calm it. Not your fault, not mine. This land was built for a horse and cart.'

'I'm not a horse and this vehicle is not a cart!'

'All right, all right!'

We tolerated each other after this shouting match. I collected the case of wine, the driver laboriously turned the van round and set off back up the lane while I went into the cottage and joined Jeannie.

'I daren't watch,' I said, sitting down on the sofa, 'he doesn't realise it'll be much worse taking the van up the lane than bringing it down!'

Thus Ambrose, because of these hazards concerning the lane, seemed safe in his private world. True, there was one occasion when a sports car, a young man in a garish shirt at the wheel, a terrified young woman beside him, raced down the lane, flew over Monty's Leap, turned left at the barn short of the cottage and shot through the gate into the stable field where it came to a stop in the middle. But this kind of driving being unique, Ambrose did not have to face serious traffic danger.

After Oliver died he showed no wish to have a companion: and any visiting cat, no doubt looking for a comfortable home, was immediately despatched off the premises. He was content to be alone with us, utterly content; and no wonder. Jeannie considered that in view of his nervous ways, his startled reaction to any unusual noise, his visible reaction of terror whenever a stranger appeared, he merited special attention. Especially in the months after Oliver died.

At the time he was a skinny cat and I would say to Jeannie that I was disappointed in him, that he looked like any ordinary cat, that although his coat was the colour of autumn bracken like Monty, he was only a pale carbon copy. Jeannie did not like me making such comments because she knew there was truth in them. He also suffered from a certain roughness along his spinal cord which thinned his fur. A visitor would look at him doubtfully, and I would find myself apologising for his appearance.

In due course our vet found a cure. A certain pill had to be mixed with his food, but it required an intuitive sense as to how much of the pill had to be given from week to week, sometimes half the pill, sometimes a quarter. Jeannie was successful in her task, so successful that Ambrose blossomed. His fur grew thick and plush and now instead of looking like a skinny ordinary cat, I was glad to admit he had become a splendid replica of Monty, resembling Monty in his lush days at Minack.

Thus, if a visitor had a glimpse of him there would be a cry of admiration; and if, by some lucky chance, Ambrose was in a dozy mood and the visitor had a camera at the ready, a photograph would be obtained of this cat who was so wary of the human race. If he wasn't dozy he would flee, and the visitor would put his camera away in disappointment.

There came a day when we particularly hoped he would be in a dozy mood; and in order to produce such a mood Jeannie had given him an especially large plate of coley as soon as we got up in the morning. For it had been arranged that a photographer from a London newspaper should come to Minack to photograph him.

The photographer had travelled by the night train from London and arrived by taxi at the cottage soon after breakfast. This was unfortunate because Ambrose, just at that moment, replete with coley, was setting off to find a suitable place to curl up and sleep. He was serenely walking down the path when the taxi arrived and the girl got out.

He flashed past her in the direction of the barn.

'Was that Ambrose?' the girl asked.

'Yes,' I replied, 'that was.'

'He's beautiful!'

I was only too well aware that we were going to have problems. The girl, I sensed, was not. She would take a few quick photographs of Ambrose, and away. I, on the other hand, knew that a sneak photograph was possible maybe, but a posed photograph impossible, except one taken by me or Jeannie.

The girl was a professional, an armour of toughness around her, yet very feminine. Slim, with long brown hair, in jeans with battledress jacket. One of the breed of newspaper photographers you see rushing, cameras hopefully pointing, as a car containing a newsworthy subject speeds away from a street kerb; or who risk their lives in danger spots around the world for those who unfold their newspapers in comfortable armchairs. Thousands of photographs taken, only the spasmodic one published.

'I love cats,' she said. 'I have one of my own and my boyfriend looks after him when I am away.'

Those who love cats, those like Jeannie, for instance, who have worshipped cats since childhood, confidently expect any cat they meet to reciprocate their love. This attitude I have always considered strange. Dog lovers can always expect their love to be immediately reciprocated by a dog, for dogs are by nature friendly. Cats, on the other hand, are aloof; and it is this aloofness which cat lovers frequently praise. So why do they behave, as I have seen Jeannie behave, in such a fawning fashion towards a cat which ignores them? (You see that there still remains a suspicious attitude towards cats and cat lovers in my subconscious.)

There was no sign of Ambrose for an hour. We searched in all his usual hiding spots, but there was no sign of him. We looked into the depths of the *escallonia* on the way to the bridge; I went up to the washing line where he sometimes

41

curled up in the grass underneath; Jeannie and I both called and called; I went in to the barn where I thought he might be hiding in the bracken which was the donkeys' bedding; no sign of Ambrose anywhere until Jeannie suddenly called out that he was on the far end of the garage roof.

'Thank goodness,' said the girl.

'I've got a bribe for him,' said Jeannie, 'I've got a plate of crab. He'll come for that.'

'My camera is ready,' said the girl.

She had remained patient during the search for Ambrose. Yet she was in a hurry.

'I've just come back from an assignment in Monte Carlo,' she had explained, 'and tomorrow I'm due to fly to Cairo. So I have to catch the afternoon train back to London.'

We had instinctively liked the girl, for within minutes of meeting there were no barriers. Except for Ambrose.

'Come on, Ambrose, come on. I've crab for you, a saucer full of crab.'

Jeannie was standing on a bank which backs onto the garage and she had placed the saucer on the flat roof of the garage.

'Come on, Ambrose.'

A minute passed, then he sneaked forward, reached the saucer and gobbled. Then away again as if hounds were chasing him.

'No good,' said the girl 'no good at all. My editor wanted a close-up.'

She was never to take it. Ambrose disappeared into the wood and we did not see him again until after the girl had left; and then we saw him sauntering up the path looking pleased with himself, a cat who had successfully blocked an intrusion into his private world.

So instead of Ambrose the girl took photographs of the donkeys. Merlin, Mingoose Merlin as he used to be known in the show ring, is an easier subject to photograph than

42

Fred. He liked to pose, an echo perhaps of his show days. He was Champion Foal at the Devon County Show, won a first prize at Penzance, was sixth in the all-comers Champion Foal class at the prestigious Stoneleigh Show. His breeder regretted that his show days ended when he came to Minack. Sometimes, I think, he regrets it himself.

Fred, on the other hand, is aloof and impervious to flattery. He will co-operate only when he is in the mood, when he is seeking a diversion to the day, and he gives the impression that he is blasé about being photographed. This was not always so. In the days when he had birthday parties, a concourse of laughing children from the school at nearby St Buryan around him, stroking him, asking for rides, giving him their ice cream, he relished being photographed among them. It is the years which have made him sedate.

On this occasion the girl had no difficulty in photographing each on their own. It was when she wanted them both together with Jeannie and I beside them that the difficulties arose, for it is a tricky task persuading two donkeys to synchronise their look at a camera.

'Could you persuade Fred to move to the right?' the girl called out to me as we stood in front of the cottage holding the donkeys by their halters; and I put a hand on Fred's haunches, shoving him.

'That's better,' the girl said. Then a moment later, 'Oh Merlin, why go that way?' Merlin had pulled at his halter and before Jeannie could stop him had lunged at a marigold.

They had many other photographs taken before the girl set off on her afternoon train. She was satisfied. She may not have been able to take a photograph of a cat, but she had two photogenic donkeys for her Sunday newspaper.

Ambrose has never been a wanderer. His territory does not go beyond the Lama field above the bridge or the wood on the other side of the donkey field; or the gate up the lane which opens upon the clover field; or the stable field in front of the barn; or the field where we have California daffodils and three hangar-like greenhouses. I have never seen him hunting further away. It is this area that is his private world.

He is a great purrer at night on our bed. I can be lying awake in the early hours, devising angry letters to send to those who may have vexed me by some action or lack of action (angry letters that I seldom write when morning comes) and my angry thoughts, as time goes by, are soothed by this wonderful sound of Ambrose's ceaseless purrs. He has always been a great purrer. When Oliver was alive he used to bash Ambrose sometimes with his paw, telling him to shut up.

Ambrose's normal custom is to sleep on the sofa until one or two in the morning; and then walk from the sofa to our bed, and if we are awake we will hear the yap of his greeting as he proceeds to snuggle close to Jeannie. After a while he will move to my side or perhaps choose to lie at the bottom of the bed upon my ankles. If I am sound asleep I do not mind because I am not aware of it, but there come those times when I am awake and I dare not move, and I fear that cramp is coming on and I still dare not move ... until the discomfort is too great and I shift my legs. Ambrose shows his displeasure at my selfishness by jumping out of the window into the night.

On early fine mornings his favourite stroll with us is the one to the Ambrose Rock. When we reach it he will jump up and break out in purrs, just as he did on that first day after we had become owners of the land. After a while, he will continue to stroll with us along the glades I have cut out from the bracken and the undergrowth, sniffing here and there, making his mark sometimes so as to prove to any possible cat trespasser that the glades are his territory. It was peaceful to be with him on these occasions, the peace people yearn for but are unable to find if they are caught in a way of life from which they cannot escape. Yet, enjoying such peace, I do not always feel free. The fears of the struggle for survival are never far from the surface.

There is another stroll we take with Ambrose called an HA (hang about). It is a very slow stroll up the lane and on a cold day we wrap up, put on an extra jersey, because Ambrose likes to linger on this stroll. He may pause because he suspects a mouse in the grass, or a frog by Monty's Leap, and when it proves to be a false alert he will continue slowly up the lane until there is another alert, and he pauses again. It is a chilly stroll on a winter morning.

One HA this spring produced a surprising incident. We had gone very slowly quite a distance up the lane, Jeannie ahead of me, Ambrose in between, when I suddenly saw peeping through the undergrowth at the side of the lane, on a track I well knew was used by the local fox family, the head of a vixen with a rabbit in her mouth. A second later the vixen dashed out of the undergrowth and leapt over Ambrose. Ambrose was amazed, and he was more amazed when he saw a dead rabbit in front of him! The vixen had dropped it.

Ambrose has never been an indoor cat during the day. He ignores the comfort of an empty bed or an empty armchair, and favours instead the donkey hay we store in the Orlyt or a small cardboard box lined with old jerseys on the bench in the small greenhouse; or he sleeps in various outdoor hideouts which we endeavour to keep track of but are always defeated by a new one. He only comes indoors in the evening; and so, after having our dinner, he proceeds to exercise his influence over us.

Since I grew up with dogs, treating cats as a matter of course as vermin, I naturally could scarcely believe that a time would come in my life when I humbly awaited a cat's decision: does he or does he not want my seat? Easy to understand Jeannie's attitude because she has been pro-cat

all her life. If, in the evening after dinner, Ambrose looks demandingly at her as she sits comfortably in her armchair in front of the fire, she will realise immediately the purpose of his stare; and so she will get up from her armchair and Ambrose will jump up in her place; and instead of sitting in a comfortable armchair she will sit on an old-fashioned milking stool. I would never have thought it possible when I was young that I would ever respond in the same fashion. Yet it happens. If Ambrose wants my corner of the sofa, I move away.

One evening there was a flood in the cottage. We were sitting reading, Jeannie on her milking stool, Ambrose in the armchair, when he began to stir, then he jumped off the armchair and prowled towards the door. I respect Ambrose when he shows such interest, as I would a guard dog. Something was afoot. Was there a menacing stranger outside?

A flood was the menacing stranger. Rain had been falling for many hours and the rainwater had built up into a lake outside the porch door, then seeped into the porch itself, and was now entering the cottage. Ambrose had given the alarm, but it was too late. Five minutes later the cottage carpet which we had possessed for many years was awash.

The consequence of the flood, however, was to our advantage, though the behaviour of Ambrose was not. Indeed his behaviour merited anyone who was anti-cat to be more anti-cat. We had recently taken up a replacement-as-new insurance policy and without enquiring how long we had had the flood-soaked carpet, the insurance company authorised us to buy a new one.

It was to cost several hundred pounds and instead of the dark green of the old carpet, we chose a myrtle-green carpet. When it was installed I was so delighted with our choice that I promised Jeannie I would Hoover it every day without being asked.

It was on the third day of this Hoovering enthusiasm that I noticed under my desk a little circle of tiny tufts. Their significance, however, did not register in my mind. I thought that the workmen responsible for laying the carpet might have made an error and, because it was under the desk, decided not to mention it to us. The following day, beside the bookcase behind my desk, I found another little circle of tiny tufts. More were to come in the following days, tiny tufts here, tiny tufts there, and then the awful truth dawned upon me. Ambrose was rotovating the beautiful myrtle-green carpet with his claws.

'Sprinkle pepper on the carpet,' we were advised by a knowledgeable friend who had suffered a similar experience.

We sprinkled pepper, we both sneezed; and Ambrose took his rotovator to another spot.

'You must try a stronger pepper,' said our friend, 'a special anti-cat pepper.'

We tried that too.

'You'll have to have his claws cut,' said another friend, 'that will be the only way to stop him.'

I was in a dilemma. A rotovated carpet or a clawless Ambrose? Jeannie was to decide.

'Ambrose clawless,' she said indignantly, 'how would he catch mice, and rabbits, and face an enemy like a fox?'

'Your decision,' I said, glad to have it made for me.

'We'll just have to try and teach him . . . shout at him as soon as he starts doing it.'

The snag was that he always rotovated at night, so that we did not see him at work. We would be sound asleep when, waking up on the sofa or the armchair, he would decide to join us. It was the interval between waking up in the early hours and joining us in bed that he chose to rotovate.

So upon our beautiful new myrtle-green carpet there is an ever-increasing number of little circles of tiny tufts.

FOUR

I have created corners in Oliver land where I have made rough seats out of a piece of wood nailed on two logs. One early morning when April scents were filling the air, bluebells and gorse, leaves of the trichocarpa and the ascania violets, the sheer freshness of growing grass and heliotrope, cow parsley and young nettles, I walked to one of these corners, aware that there would be no man-made noise or action to disturb me. A swallow might surprise me by its earliness, so too a red admiral butterfly; and there might be the monotonous call of a chiff-chaff or the sharp

trill of a white-throat, even the sound of the first cuckoo calling away on Carn Barges . . . but, except for the murmur of a fishing boat, there would be no reminder of Man's version of civilisation.

There I was one morning, sitting on one of my seats which we jokingly called the *intime* because it is so small that two people must sit very close together, and I found myself thinking how much of my life had been spent looking for Svengalis.

When a boy, my mind seemed to be in a prison and I searched desperately for someone to open the cell door. I wanted someone to awaken my dormant desire to study literature, tell me which books I should read and what I should look for in them. This, in retrospect, sounds such a simple ambition, easily achieved, and the more so since I was being expensively educated at Harrow. Yet there was an invisible barrier between me and anyone who could have helped me, and I found no master who saw me as a boy who craved enlightenment.

My home life might have solved my problems because both my father and mother were highly intelligent, and yet here again was an invisible barrier. Books, it seemed, belonged to a special compartment in their lives and we never had general discussions about them. Conversation was limited to everyday practical matters and comments about the behaviour of people we knew; and in the evening we spent our time at the billiard table or playing a card game called Galloping Patience. There was never a flight into the realms of imagination and I never heard the work of literary figures discussed.

My father was very affectionate and, in a family concept of the description, was a saint. His life was spent in trying to sustain the financial existence of the family by pushing his own physical strength to the limit and without letting himself enjoy any personal luxuries. He adored my mother, and he believed every sacrifice on his part was justified if it secured her financial future. As for me, he was always kind and generous, and yet here again was this invisible barrier which thwarted me from having an entry into his worldly and literary knowledge.

He was able, however, to convey to me his love of music, especially of opera because when I was a child he used to take me to the Cologne Opera House where, at that time, Otto Klemperer and Bruno Walter were resident conductors; and so my being was absorbed by Wagner and Puccini and Verdi. This was my father's gift to me, but there still remained this invisible barrier.

I believe it was due to shyness on both our parts, and that it was shyness on my part that also caused this invisible barrier between me and other people. One of the consequences of shyness is that it can give the impression that you are being offhand, or rude, or dull. It is not, however, only with strangers that you can give this misleading impression. You can give it sometimes to someone close to you when, to your bewilderment, you find the words you want to say remain gagged in your mind. Another form of shyness is when you talk too much just to cover up your shyness and you sound silly and trivial; and later, when you look back on the occasion you know you have let yourself down.

It was my silent shyness, however, which let me down when I was with my father. He and I shared an enthusiasm for trout fishing and we would go off together to the Fowey River near Bodmin Road station. Having parked the car and put on our waterproof leggings, we would walk to the nearby wood store and pass though the gate to the river. There we would set up our rods and tackle and select a fly which seemed suitable for the day and the time of year, and then begin to cast our lines. I was a schoolboy but already I preferred to be a solitary person. So did my father. We would fish a quarter of a mile apart.

It was the car journey to the Fowey River, however, which provided the opportunity to talk. But we only chatted, and that was all. Yet my father would suddenly show his affection for me by putting a hand on my knee as he drove and murmuring: 'Dear Cur.' The word 'Cur' was one of those incomprehensible family endearments which are a cover for the middleclass who, though wishing to show affection, feel embarrassed by doing so. 'Cur' was indeterminate. The name Derek was too definitive.

I always knew, therefore, that my father was on my side and every now and then he would bestow on me a snatch of wisdom which was to live with me always. For instance, one evening I was with him on a Cornish cliff marvelling at a sunset, and I began to analyse the colours. He broke in and stopped me.

'Enjoy the sunset,' he said, 'don't analyse it. Too much analysing destroys the pleasure of magic.'

This shyness haunted me, holding me back in my growing up. There came a teenage time, for instance, when I was looking for a girl Svengali, and when, in due course, I thought I had found her, I went back one evening to her home. She opened the door with her latchkey and as we entered I saw an envelope on the floor. The girl picked it up, then I followed her into the sitting-room where she opened the envelope and began to read. For some minutes, or it seemed to me at the time to be some minutes, she stared at the notepaper, and as she did so my shyness displayed itself. I jumped to the conclusion that it was a love letter and that, although I believed I had found my girl Svengali, she belonged to someone else. I lost my nerve, murmured a goodbye and left. Two or three years later I met her again and because I was now emotionally free of her, I was able with detachment to refer to that occasion when she took me back to her home. I asked who the letter was from. It was from someone of no importance to her. She had stood looking at the letter, not reading it, waiting for action on my part. My shyness had denied me my girl Svengali.

Soon after this failure I did indeed meet a Svengali in the form of an Egyptian diplomat who frequented the Grosvenor House ice rink; and he proved to be a Svengali who was to influence me for the rest of my life. He was an authority on Marcel Proust, the great French writer whose *Remembrance of Things Past* he told me to read. This was to be the key to the cell door. As we skated around the rink my Egyptian friend told me that I would find out about the subtleties of human relationships which, in real life, would take me years to find out; and that again and again I would discover dormant thoughts of my own. Proust, he said, wrote as an observer of people's whims and contradictions, and he went on to say that I would find reassurance in many passages because I would discover that thoughts, doubts and fears which inexperience made me believe were exclusively my own, were also shared by others.

My erudite Egyptian friend (he wrote a classic book in the thirties about Proust) told me that when the first volume, *Swann's Way*, appeared, some reviewers objected to the manner Proust wrote in the first person, alleging that it was a form of narcissism. On the contrary, explained my Egyptian friend, it was a literary device. It made him feel freer and by using it Proust believed that his readers, as if they were looking in a mirror, would see their own selves reflected.

This was indeed the impression that it made on me. Not long ago I was invited to be the castaway on Desert Island Discs and when at the end of the programme I was asked by Roy Plomley the customary question as to what book I would like to have on my desert island, I replied that *Remembrance of Things Past* would be my choice. I had first read the work in the Scott Moncrieff translation, but there had recently been a new translation which I wanted to obtain. After receiving my fee for being a castaway, I walked down to Hatchards, the famous bookshop in Piccadilly, and bought all three volumes of the Kilmartin translation, a massive three thousand pages.

I read Proust now with a different view of its contents but the first time, the time when my Egyptian friend introduced me to Proust, I found as a young man in and out of love that the contents of *Remembrance of Things Past* were a revelation. Here was an author of worldly experience explaining the behaviour of other people, of girls in particular for me at that age, in words that I could understand; and I would frequently find a sentence which would contribute to the erosion of my feelings of inadequacy, however temporary that erosion might prove to be.

For instance, I had an inferiority complex because of my failure to pass my school examinations ('you're useless to society,' my Harrow housemaster had told me) and I used to be depressed when I read articles and books in which words flowed so cleverly and freely, yet which appeared to me to contain little meaning. I was sure it must be a fault of mine and I blamed this lack of understanding on my scholastic failures.

Then one day I read a sentence in which Proust is referring to a character of high intellectual reputation and that sentence released me from my inferiority complex. It read: 'Like many intellectuals he was incapable of saying anything in a simple way.'

I was, however, at this period, more interested in his dissertations about the waywardness of the girls he fell in love with, or was tempted to fall in love with. These dissertations fascinated me as I believe they would fascinate introvert thinking people of any period. The perplexities which bewildered me were the same as those of Proust, first with his Gilberte, then Albertine; and to show such perplexities do not end when you are young but continue with you as you grow older, there is the intricate story of Swann's love for Odette. For anyone frustrated in love I recommend the volume in *Rememberance of Things Past* called *Swann's Way*; for here you will recognise the jealousies, the sudden raptures, the inexplicable behaviour of the loved one; or the inexplicable behaviour of yourself when, if an opportunity presents itself, action is blocked by inertia. Nothing is black or white in Proust's story of love.

None the less I have sometimes regretted Proust's influence over me because, as a result, I am inclined to imagine thoughts going through another person's mind which are not in fact there. This makes me hesitant when I should be bold. I fail to take action because I fear that the nonexistent thoughts are against it. Yet I cannot blame Proust: he opened up my mind. I blame myself.

Jeannie, too, has looked for Svengalis. She looked for one after she had completed the manuscript of *Meet Me At The Savoy*, and after several disappointments she found one in the person of the managing director of a small publishing firm. Larger publishing firms had turned down her manuscript, but the managing director of this small firm was ecstatic in his enthusiasm. And this enthusiasm has long since been justified, for *Meet Me At The Savoy* has become an autobiographical classic.

She did not begin writing again for some while, and then the idea slowly developed in her mind of writing a novel which traced the story of a great London hotel from the war years to the present day. When she wrote *Meet Me At The Savoy* I used to lock her in a hut, the hut where we used to bunch violets and which, in due course, was joined to the cottage and became the spare bedroom. I used to leave her there for a couple of hours before letting her out – and if this sounds harsh I must explain that the locking-up was done with her permission. She knew that if she was to complete the book she had to be cut off from outside temptations.

The working habit on her first novel, called *Hotel Regina*, came under a different category of discipline. There was no urgency to complete it. She was embarking on a long journey and she realised there would be three novels, a trilogy, before her story would end. She could take her time. In a way, what she was setting out to do was a form of indulgence. She had a belief in the story she was to tell and its completion to her personal satisfaction would be her reward.

None the less, personal satisfaction likes also to be recognised in kind, and so Jeannie sent away two manuscript copies of this first of the trilogy, one to a well-known agent and one to a publisher who had from the first encouraged her in her project. Neither Jeannie nor I will ever forget the day when their replies were received.

'Unpublishable,' said the agent in effect.

'Very disappointed,' said the publisher, 'my fiction editor advises us not to publish it.'

Many hopeful writers have had similar experiences, just as many of them have later proved a publisher very wrong in his judgment. But when these letters arrived I watched Jeannie's despair and thought of the injustice that a beautiful book had been treated with such disdain. So, without telling her, I got into the car, raced into Penzance and bought a bottle of champagne.

Then, on my return, I asked her to come to the hut in the wood where she had spent so many hours writing *Hotel Regina*. Outside the hut door I had placed the bottle of champagne and attached a note to it. On the note was an old 'Cornish' phrase which was intended to make her laugh. And it did!

Her disappointment did not last long because another publisher, a famous publisher, accepted the book and when it was published it was hailed as being on the same level as Arnold Bennett's *Imperial Palace*. When its successor, *Home is the Hotel*, second of the trilogy, was published a reviewer on the BBC talked about it as being far better than Vicki Baum's *Grand Hotel*. So Jeannie had both her personal satisfaction as a reward and the admiration of those who read books.

A month before this moment when I was sitting on the seat we jokingly called *intime*, Jeannie had received a telegram (one of the last it proved to be before telegrams were assigned to history) from her publisher about the third of the trilogy which she called *Bertioni's Hotel*. It was a busy day in the daffodil season. Margaret and Joan were bunching, Jeannie was packing the blooms in their cardboard boxes, while I was tying them up and carrying them to the Volvo. I was in a rush. I had to reach the lorries leaving Long Rock on the other side of Penzance before 2 pm.

Just as I was setting off, down the lane in his car came our friend Leslie Payne, who was then the local postmaster at St Buryan. It was part of the charm of Leslie that when he delivered a telegram he would hint at its contents before we had time to open the envelope. Thus, if it was sad news he would say, as he handed the telegram: 'Sorry about this', or if it was good news he would say brightly: 'This will be a happy day for you!'

Anyone who has experienced the instant when a great endeavour has been acclaimed, is aware that such a moment will probably prove to be the most exciting, the happiest of all. In the case of a book I am sure it is true. That moment when the news comes that it has been accepted, when the mental turmoil, the sleepless nights, the self-discipline and determination needed to overcome those periods when one is bereft of ideas . . . that one moment when all of it has been proved worthwhile, is the Everest moment.

'*Bertioni's Hotel* splendid,' said the telegram, 'letter and offer following.'

Charmingly Margaret and Joan rushed to kiss her, while I, needing to get away with the daffodil boxes as quickly as possible, getting into the car, turning on the engine, I said to Jeannie we would celebrate on my return. And so we did.

She was waiting for me in front of the cottage.

'What do you think I've been doing? I've been going round Oliver land, talking out loud, saying, "Oh gosh, oh gosh!"'

It was an unusual expression for Jeannie to use, and yet its simplicity mirrored her character. She was able to mix easily with people from any walk of life because success has never been a desire to satisfy vanity. She has achieved it unaffectedly. Yet there is an aspect of her which is significant: she is only at her best, in career terms, with top people. She understands their language. She is at a loss, however, when dealing with the unimaginative, and she becomes unsure of herself. But when she deals with top people she intuitively plays their game, to her advantage and theirs. It is as if she is playing on the Centre Court at Wimbledon.

I left the seat we call *intime* where I had been ruminating and began slowly to walk round the most faraway part of Oliver land. The grass path was barely a foot wide, bluebells crowding either side, and the tiny flowers of the stitchwort were scattered among them. Infant bracken was beginning to show, their fronds curled, resembling a baby's fist. Gorse, their cushions of golden petals hiding the spiky leaves, at intervals, wafted their scent. A lark was singing above the fields inland to my left and to my right among the scrubland a whitethroat burst into a frenzied chattering. I looked for it and saw it perched on a bramble; and I marvelled that this tiny bird, which a few weeks before was in North Africa, had now taken up its summer home on a Cornish cliff.

It is an incident like that which makes me want to worship not God but Creation. God may be a symbol for mankind to worship but mankind, it seems to me, has misused the symbol. Mankind expects too much of God. It is absurd, for instance, for two opposing sides to pray to God for their success. It is absurd, also, to believe that God is omnipotent. For if this is so all the unfairness in the world, whether it is famine, chronic illness of a child, violence, poverty, cruelty or any other miserable condition, is attributable to God. I find it difficult to accept the excuse of theologians that God sends these horrors to test us.

Mankind has also, I believe, misused the symbol of God by involving God in politics, by exciting competition among different religions, producing animosity as a result, so that instead of love there is hate, instead of peace there is war. How many religious wars have there been in history? How many are in progress today? God, it seems to me, is used as an alibi by those who wish to legitimise their ambitions.

I am puzzled, also, by the theoretical rigmarole of those clerics who place such importance on how a sentence in a prayer book or a hymn is written. Such dogma appears to be the antithesis of what God, in the beginning, was supposed to be. God, in the beginning, was all-embracing, not narrow-minded. Nor do I understand why we, the congregation, should in Church services cringe in our prayers, murmuring 'we miserable sinners' etc. These cringing words are Man-made. It is as if the Church hierarchy feels it is necessary for us all to have this cringing humility. But why? The mystique of God is, I believe, once again being made use of by mankind. For it seems that personal ambitions dominate many connected with religious affairs. The preservation of religious power is more important than evoking God's simplicity.

Thus, as I wandered on Oliver land, peace around me, the surging mood of spring, the horizon-stretched expanse of a restless sea, the agelessness of the grey granite rocks lying half-hidden by the greening undergrowth, I was thinking that God should be freed from being used by mankind; and instead there should be worship of Creation. Creation is anything that moves, anything that scents, anything that is magical, anything that logic cannot explain, it is anything as ethereal as courage and kindness; and it is anything that inspires music, art, beauty. Creation can be worshipped without anyone meddling. Creation is what God was in the beginning.

I reached the most distant point of Oliver land, which we call Candy Corner because the donkeys find grass and pink campion there of particular delicacy, and if they accompany us on a walk they will always stop at Candy Corner, leaving us to continue on our way. There is a stunted hawthorn there with honeysuckle twined around it and in summer, as we pass it, the air is full of honeysuckle scents. The hawthorn grows among brambles and the donkeys cannot reach it, and this is fortunate because the donkeys devour the honeysuckle with the same greed as some people devour asparagus.

There was, for instance, an area further on from Candy Corner, and which I was soon to reach in my wander around Oliver land, that with no originality we called Honeysuckle Corner. I had discovered it when I was opening up the paths in Oliver land with the heavy Condor rotary mowing machine. I had charged down a slope through a forest of bracken then alongside a waist-high dry-stone wall hemming in an ancient overgrown meadow, and suddenly I was faced by a sprawling mass of honeysuckle. I swerved round it and continued on my way, and hastened to tell Jeannie about it when I returned to the cottage. For a while we relished walking to Honeysuckle Corner, standing there, drinking in the scent, and we would tell friends to walk there, and they too would relish the experience. Then, alas, the donkeys discovered it as they wandered round in the freedom of Oliver land and that was the end of Honeysuckle Corner.

The donkeys are, in fact, vandals.

'Look at that vandal Fred,' I will say to Jeannie, as Fred takes a swipe at a clump of primroses. He has a passion for primroses.

'Stop it, Merlin,' I will shout, as he gnaws at the bark of a hawthorn.

There is no doubt that they have hindered the development of Oliver land in the way we wanted to develop it. There was no purpose in opening up the land for agricultural or horticultural crops because the expense of doing so would be far greater than the receipts. So we decided to plant trees in strategic places to enhance the landscape. First I planted a row of *olearia*, and they disappeared as soon as the donkeys caught sight of them. Then I planted a hundred hawthorn saplings, dotting them around the place. Certainly some of them died naturally, but there were many which were Merlin's victims. Merlin would find a sapling and slowly eat it, the sapling dangling from his mouth like a strand of spaghetti.

I should I suppose, be enraged by their behaviour yet,

although I will be irritated when I catch them in the act, this is not so. I should also perhaps be more practical. Instead of letting them wander at will I should corral them in the clover field or the Clarence meadow. This would be a sensible step to take, but Jeannie and I are aware that we would deny ourselves a great deal of pleasure. For there are two special pleasures that the donkeys give us on Oliver land.

There are the walks of course, though our presence does not necessarily mean they will accompany us. Our routine is for them to be in the stable field or the donkey field close to the cottage at night and then in the morning we take them back to Oliver land. It is then that a walk with them may take place. We will tie up the gate of the clover field after letting them into it and begin a walk up the side of the field towards the blackthorn path which leads to our badger sett, then on to the Ambrose Rock. Sometimes they will ignore us, going instead to the centre of the field where they will have a roll, a donkey bath. At other times they will wait until we are out of sight, and we may have reached the site of the badger sett when we hear a pounding of hooves and the donkeys will appear, rushing up to us as if they were saying we were walking too fast. Usually they just follow us, languidly, pausing to eat their favourite morsels on the way, and often when we reach the Ambrose Rock, Fred will go up to it and proceed to lick it.

The second special pleasure they give us is when we watch them on Oliver land from the bridge, the patio close to the cottage which, with its view of Mounts Bay, gives the impression that it is the bridge of a ship. We will be standing there, looking across the valley, and Jeannie may say to me: 'I can't see the donkeys ... oh yes I can, they're in their summer house!'

She would be untruthful. She could not, in fact, see them, but she knew from experience that the sudden violent shaking of the branches of an elder tree not far from

Honeysuckle Corner meant that the donkeys were in the shade of the elder, rubbing their backs against a branch.

There was also the fun of watching them graze in the clover field, peaceful happy donkeys, always close to each other, until a sudden boredom sets in and then one suggests to the other that a walk elsewhere on Oliver land would be a good idea. Thus we may observe a change of direction on the other side of the valley. Fred has decided to move to the Clarence meadow, informed Merlin, and they follow each other through the gap, then start to munch the change of grass menu. Or they may decide to pass through the Clarence meadow, go left over four small rocks which I am always meaning to move, then along the paths I have created, a long walk perhaps, past the Ambrose Rock and beyond to Candy Corner, and then back, slowly, slowly, munching all the while, until they return via the badger sett, then along the blackthorn path to the clover field. Up there we have watched them. Not all the time. It takes half a day or more for them to make such a tour.

Their movements absorb us in other ways. On fine days rabbits appear on the clover field, and when Merlin is suffering from a period of boredom he will put his nose to the ground and chase a rabbit. I have even, on one occasion, seen him chase a fox.

Another diversion for both Fred and Merlin centres around the cattle of a neighbouring farm, one field of which is divided by a low stone hedge from a section of gorse-covered patches of Oliver land, gorgeously interspersed by carpets of bluebells. On the day before that morning I was wandering after sitting ruminating on the *intime* seat, Fred and Merlin had met a concourse of young bullocks from this neighbouring farm for the first time. Or perhaps I should say this the other way round. The bullocks saw Fred and Merlin for the first time.

The attitude of Fred and Merlin was one of great dignity.

They took up their positions on their side of the hedge, the bullocks on the other side. The bullocks jostled together in excitement while Fred and Merlin proceeded to stare at the hysterical youngsters like pop stars might stare at a mob of hysterical fans. Fred and Merlin clearly enjoyed the adulation for they stayed there accepting the applause for a quarter of an hour or more and then, deciding that their public had received their money's worth, they leisurely departed.

At other periods of the year cows sometimes replace bullocks on this neighbouring field and then similar meetings take place between them and Fred and Merlin, though on a more solemn level. Instead of the snuffling noises of an hysterical youthful mob, serious conversations seem to occur. A cow will come up to her side of the hedge, Fred on his side, and they will stare at each other, a large cow nose a short distance away from Fred's white nose. While their conversation is in progress, another cow, perhaps a younger one, is communicating with Merlin.

This herd of cows has an unusual leader, a donkey by the name of Duncan. Duncan is not unlike Fred, with a coffee-coloured coat and being larger than the conventional grey donkey. Duncan is recognised by his farmer owner as having a very strong character, and from our look-out point on the bridge Jeannie and I have witnessed this to be true.

There are, apart from the field adjacent to Oliver land, interlocking fields which belong to the farmer, open gaps joining them, and we have often seen Duncan become tired of the field he is in and proceed to go through a gap into another. Promptly, the cows follow him. He is the leader. They must obey.

Duncan, however, has caused his owner some problems. He is, in donkey tradition, a Houdini as far as gates are concerned and he has used his gifts to lead his ladies on some remarkable escapades. On two occasions, for instance, just as the Wink, the pub at Lamorna, was about to close at night, Bob and Di Drennan, the landlords, have found Duncan and all his ladies milling around at the door. Duncan, having unlatched a farmgate, had led them half a mile down a lane to get there by closing-time!

The relationship between him and Fred and Merlin is distant though cordial. I have the impression, however, when watching Duncan from the bridge that he considers himself superior. After all he is the leader of a herd of cows, a donkey with responsibility ... 'What do *you* do,' he seems to be saying as he looks at Fred and Merlin from the other side of the hedge.

They, in their turn, sometimes seem to behave like juniors in an office who want to curry favour with a senior. They will catch sight of Duncan in the field and they will turn from the path, walk between the gorse bushes to the hedge, and stand there, hopefully. Unfortunately Duncan often ignores them. Then I have also seen Duncan snub them, as a host might snub a guest who bores him. A dialogue between the donkeys would seem to be successfully in progress when I have seen Duncan suddenly turn away, leaving Fred and Merlin standing there bewildered. 'What have we done?'

I have digressed from the impressions of that early morning walk around Oliver land, digressed after reaching Honeysuckle Corner which the donkeys have so unfortunately demolished. A substantial bush of honeysuckle, however, is now saved because it is within the ancient, overgrown meadow adjacent to Honeysuckle Corner. We have made it impossible for the donkeys to enter it. Ambrose, when he is on a walk with us, will enter it, jumping up on the hedge and down again. Then he will make his way to the wood seat I have made in a corner and he will sit there, in the shape of a Trafalgar lion, looking magnificent; and because it is always early morning when we walk with Ambrose to Oliver land, the rising sun shines upon his rich autumn-bracken-coloured coat. He sits there, blinking.

I reached this point on my walk and could not make up my mind whether to take the path I had made to my right, towards the Clarence meadow, or continue forwards to the thickly covered copse we had named the Brontë wood. We had named it so because there is a connection between the wild Cornish cliffs and Haworth. Maria Branwell had her home in Chapel Street, Penzance, and from number 25 she set off to Yorkshire to marry Patric Brontë.

I finally decided to take the path to the Brontë wood.

FIVE

Ahead of me as I walked toward the Brontë wood was a small gorsebush around which the path curved, and I had nearly reached it when, from the other side of the gorsebush, I heard a small growl erupting into a soft 'woof', a sound like that of a puppy. I thought of the new arrival at the farm at the top, a brown and white spaniel called Trigger, but I quickly realised it could not be him because Trigger though young was no longer a puppy. Then, a second later, I rounded the gorsebush and saw the instigator of the 'woof'. It was a fox cub, a toddler, who trundled off into the undergrowth as soon as he saw me.

I continued along the path towards the Brontë wood, knee-high bluebells on either side of me, buttercups and pink campion, and stitchwort, and patches of sorrel. It was quiet except for the sudden clap of a courting pigeon, the clap of its wings as it dived towards another, and the clear song of a blackbird declaring its love for life from an elder tree to my right. I could hear, too, a buzzard mewing high in the sky and gulls spasmodically engaging in a harsh conversation down on the rocks to my left. I had now reached the edge of the Brontë wood and the path that leads narrowly into it, making one feel one is entering a tunnel. Not a narrow tunnel. It is a canopy of a tunnel, branches of long-established elders serving as a top, darkening below, so that one walks on earth instead of grass.

I was just about to enter the wood when I froze.

Just in front of me was a gull. It was perky in that I could not have said: 'Oh dear, here is a sick gull!' Instead, at the sight of me it ran away fast into the inside of the wood, at the speed of a running pheasant.

I hesitated for a moment before following it. I tried to figure out what could have happened. Presumably, as it could run but could not fly, it must have had a broken wing, yet I had seen no sign of one: a broken wing usually droops. In any case what possible reason could there be for a gull to choose such a place to hide?

I was about to follow when I remembered an incident which had taken place a few days previously. I had been meandering with the donkeys and in the process of this meandering they had led me to a May tree, standing on its own a few yards outside the Brontë wood, and where they scratched their backs on one of its lower branches. When I joined them I noticed a scattering of white feathers on the ground, and although I at first thought they were chicken feathers, I soon realised they were the feathers of a gull. Obviously the victim of a fox.

So, remembering this, I left my gull in the wood and walked over to have another look around the May tree. What I now found were not just the remnants of a single gull, but instead a carpet of feathers, evidence pointing to a fox's dining-room. Clearly the earth was nearby and the vixen, as is the usual custom when cubs are old enough to move away from the earth, had chosen this spot beneath the May tree as an ideal place for them to have their meals; and it now seemed that a speciality of their menu was the devouring of gulls.

I was puzzled. How had my gull escaped from being part of the menu? How was it that the vixen was allowing the gull to run free within such a short distance of her dining-room? How had it come to be here? Was it just coincidence that it had damaged a wing then landed within a few yards of the dining-room? Or had it been caught by the vixen while roosting sleepily on a rock close to the sea, and having been caught had been carried by her to the dining-room, then miraculously had escaped?

There are some people who desire a logical explanation for every mystery. Their tidy minds require reasons for anything they cannot immediately understand. For instance, there are many who are sceptical of faith healers, but although I have not personally experienced such a healer, far too many people have told me of their experiences for me not to believe in their magical achievements.

There is a soldier I know whose back had been broken and who, under conventional treatment, recovered sufficiently to walk with a stick. Then complications set in. A few months later he was only able to crawl about the house and conventional doctors said they could do no more for him. Then a friend sent a healer to him and a few days later he was walking normally. A similar experience occurred to the wife of a friend of mine. She was in her early thirties but Harley Street doctors warned her she would soon be bedridden. Reluctantly she was persuaded to go to a healer who lived in Torquay, and there the magic took place. She now plays golf and rides, and leads a normal life.

The acceptance of magic, however, requires a special attitude, a fey attitude, an attitude which digital-minded people find difficult to understand. They have been trained to expect a logical answer to any problem and so they are impatient with those of us who believe in magic, who believe that much of our lives are governed by forces that have nothing to do with logic; and, for that matter, govern the life of a gull. For there is no logical explanation for what happened after I left Brontë wood to return to the cottage.

The gull had disappeared deep into the wood and its only way out was along the foot-wide path which I proceeded to take on my way back to the cottage. After about a hundred yards the path bore left, and then it ran parallel to the hedge which bordered the Clarence meadow. At the far end, where the Clarence meadow joined the clover field, was a narrow gap in which there were the four half-submerged rocks which I constantly intend to move but never do. Hence one has to walk gingerly through this gap, both humans and donkeys, and once through one turns right into the broad expanse of the clover field and, on the far side, there is the sight of the gate which leads into the lane.

It was a Friday and on Friday mornings Jeannie goes into Penzance to perform the weekly shopping. She leaves around eight in the morning and there have been occasions, when the weather has been rough and Jeannie has reluctantly said goodbye, that I have retreated back to bed because Ambrose, snug amongst the blankets, has lured me. Not, of course, on this morning, a lovely morning, when any romantic would feel as I did. A sense of wonder for everything that is not conceived by Man.

I hurried and I was back in the cottage within four minutes ... four minutes ... and as I arrived Jeannie came down the lane in the Volvo.

'Guess what I've just seen,' she said excitedly, and I, impatient to tell her my story, had to wait. 'As I came down the lane, halfway there was a gull in front of me, and it didn't fly away, it just ran!'

I looked at her in astonishment.

'I can't believe you,' I said, 'I've just left a gull like that in the Brontë wood!'

Then I told her what had happened.

'It can't be the same gull,' I said, 'there is no means of it reaching the lane except by the route I took. And there is the time element. Even if it had gone some other way, and that would mean it had to climb two high hedges, I can't see how it possibly could have reached halfway up the lane between the last time I saw it going into the wood and the time you saw it.'

'Two gulls running about instead of flying, all within five minutes!'

'Bewildering,' I said.

'What shall we do?'

'Go looking for them.'

'Wait a moment while I feed Ambrose.'

It was customary for Ambrose to have chopped liver on Fridays as soon as Jeannie had returned. He would appear when he heard the arrival of the car and wait for Jeannie to get out, then follow her into the cottage where she would unwrap the messy liver. Ambrose miaowing with impatience. Then she would place the saucer on a newspaper, acting as a tablecloth, on the carpet and the miaowing would cease.

'I'm ready.'

We set off to go to the Brontë wood, up the lane, and to the gate that leads into the clover field; and when we reached the gate we saw, in the middle of the field, a gull. Which gull?

Jeannie, on such occasions, is inclined to take command. I may suggest a line of action, but she will go her own way. One of my earliest memories of her as press officer was the assured manner with which she treated the British and American press at a Pilgrim's Dinner at the Savoy Hotel when Sir Winston Churchill was the speaker. She, though very young, handled these tough media people so easily, and yet her authority was not derived from a feminist kind of attitude. Her strength came from her femininity.

Her femininity, however, can madden me. It is beguiling, full of opposites, emotions swinging on a pendulum, suggesting the existence of well-kept secrets, provocative in the sense that I am sometimes aware that I am being led in a direction that I do not want to go. Femininity represents the wiles of women since the beginning of time, the reason for their power over men, and so it is difficult to understand why the strident feminist of today is so keen to surrender it.

The gull was squatting as if on a nest and the buttercups in the field provided the edge to the nest so that the head of the gull was clearly to be seen while its body was half-hidden by the buttercups.

We discussed what to do. We could either leave it undisturbed or else stalk it, trying to catch it so that if the wing was broken we could take it to the Bird Hospital at Mousehole. Either choice entailed a risk: if we left it in the middle of the field, powerless to fly, it would be at the mercy of a fox when dusk came; and if we tried to catch it it might run away, we would not know where it had gone and it would be even easier prey for a fox.

I was in a state of indecision, the Pisces influence under which I was born, two fishes swimming each way, dithering because the advantages and disadvantages appear to be equal on both sides of a problem.

'I will go to the left,' said Jeannie, 'and you go to the right. Then we will both advance towards it, and if he is in a bad state he won't move, and we will catch him ...'

'Darling,' I said, 'I don't think this will work. We will frighten it. Let's go back to the bridge and watch through fieldglasses, and take time to map out a plan of campaign. It's only morning. There's a long time to dusk.'

We proceeded to go about our business, every now and then going up to the bridge and staring across the valley to the white spot which was the gull. It did not move. Jeannie's business was more enjoyable than mine. I was coping with accounts while Jeannie was going through the photographs of movie stars she had amassed over the years, photographs they have given her. She had been asked to make an inventory of them in view of the rebirth of these stars through their movies being shown on television. She had a remarkable collection, all of which used to adorn the walls of Room 205 at the Savoy, but, because she is un-methodical, natural, many of her photographs have been lost.

She sat at the table in the porch, a large cardboard box beside her, sorting them out. There was one of the lovely gentle Carole Landis who was to commit suicide because of frustrated love for a famous film star womaniser – 'Jean dear, thank you and bless you' is written on it in green ink. There were others inscribed to her from Ronald Colman, Laurel and Hardy, Bing Crosby, Bob Hope, John Steinbeck, Ingrid Bergman, Merle Oberon and Tyrone Power. (I knew Ty before Jeannie met him: I once spent three days in Panama with him, collecting hangovers in nightclubs.) There was one from Elizabeth Taylor at the time she was about to marry her first husband, son of the founder of the Hilton hotels. Another of James Mason, as cat-loving as Jeannie, who told her that she would never be able to convert me from being anti-cat. James, when we last saw him in London, offered me a cigarette, a fat cigarette with no marking on it, and a rich Turkish aroma. 'A Sullivan,' he explained, 'the cigarette that caught Raffles.' E. V. Hornung, creator of Raffles, smoked Sullivans himself, and saw that Raffles did so too. Hence the tell-tale aroma pervading a room where Raffles had been at his criminal work, and his consequent exposure.

There were several photographs of Gertrude Lawrence with Yul Brynner in the Broadway production of *The King and I*. She had written to us after the first night: 'I think of you both even in my busiest and most nerve-racking days, and during rehearsals and the road tryout, and I have often envied your peaceful meadows. You will go wild about the play.' There was another one of her in the Daphne du Maurier play *September Tide*, and in the background is Bryan Forbes who played her son. We went to a party that Gertie gave for the cast, and Jeannie always remembers the long conversation she had that evening with Bryan Forbes. He was saying what a marvellous help Gertie had been to him, always encouraging him. Like all of us who knew Gertie he was appalled by Julie Andrews' interpretation of her in the film *Star*.

Then there was a photograph of Danny Kaye in his Walter Mitty character of a Wing Commander in the RAF. Danny wrote the foreword to *Meet Me At The Savoy*, writing it one evening in his dressing-room at the London Palladium. He also was one of those who said he owed a great deal to Gertie Lawrence. She was starring in the musical play *Lady in the Dark* on Broadway and Danny was an unknown in awe of her. He was terrified on the first night when he had to sing a song just before her big number. It was one of his nonsensical songs with the words all mixed up. He brought the house down and was called back repeatedly to the stage. His success was such that he was scared as to how Gertie would react. Stars can be very jealous of successful unknowns. Not Gertie: she asked the management to put Danny's name up in lights.

Danny asked Jeannie to be his guest at his last appearance at the Palladium, the occasion of the Royal Variety Performance to celebrate the Queen Mother's eightieth birthday. He was nervous beforehand. He was nervous because he knew that his particular act required time to work up and he didn't think he had been given enough time. He had to wait in his dressing-room as act followed act, but Danny need not have worried. He was a huge success, and when Jeannie left the theatre with him crowds stormed the Rolls, calling for Danny to come back soon for a show of his own, nostalgic calls, remembering the days when he conquered London.

Each time we went up to the bridge and looked across to the clover field there was still no movement from the gull. We had not made up our minds what to do. It was in obvious danger because we had seen cubs playing in the neighbouring Clarence meadow, and the vixen had been with them and sometimes the dog fox. Dog foxes are supposed to take no interest in family life, although there are some naturalists who say that this is not true. I can tell, too, of one strange incident which I witnessed involving a dog fox and a vixen which supports the view of the minority.

It occurred one morning in early May when I suddenly heard the hyena-like bark of a fox not far away. I hurried up to the bridge, looked across the valley and saw a fox, a huge fox, sitting upright on top of the hedges which line the Clarence meadow. The fox was staring intently across the

clover field towards the gate which leads to the lane. It looked very anxious, and periodically it let out its hyena-like barks.

Had it been a few weeks later I would have guessed it was a vixen, calling back her cubs who had gone a-roaming, but it was too early in the summer for them to be on their own. The fox continued to bark, unperturbed that he was bringing such attention upon himself in broad daylight. I waited and watched. Then came the explanation. From the direction of the clover field gate, there hurried a much smaller fox. It was a vixen, late home from hunting. The dog fox leapt down and joined her and they set off together towards the Brontë wood and the cliff.

It was nearing tea-time when we decided to act about the gull. Each time we looked at it through the fieldglasses, it had seemed somnolent, its head just appearing above the buttercups and the grass.

'The forecast is rain before evening,' I said, 'so we had better put our plan into action.'

We are lucky to have the Mousehole Bird Hospital a little over a quarter of an hour away. Founded by the remarkable Yglesias sisters it was taken over for a while by the RSPCA, then discarded by them and it is now once again sustained by voluntary subscriptions. It is not easy for the small staff. Funds are always short. Hours are long. But it remains, whatever day of the week, a haven for sick and injured birds. If we caught the gull, we planned to take it there.

'I'm ready when you are,' said Jeannie.

I proceeded to collect an empty cardboard winecase and placed hay in the bottom. Then we both put on jackets and gardening gloves because the gull, not knowing that our intentions were kind and that if he co-operated he would soon be safe in the comfort of the Bird Hospital, might object to our efforts to catch him and attack us. I also collected an old blanket with the idea that it might be necessary to throw it over the gull when we got near to it. Thus armed, we set off up the lane to the clover field.

We had decided that I should go round the edge of the field and come towards the gull from behind. Jeannie, meanwhile, would advance from the lane side. We would have to move quickly because there might be only the one chance to catch it. If we missed it the first time, it would probably go into a panic and race away.

And that is what happened. At a signal we both began to advance. We reached within a few feet. I had the rug ready temporarily to smother it . . . then away it ran. No sound, no sign of an injured wing. Away at speed.

'I expected that to happen,' said Jeannie.

'Oh well, we did our best.'

We did our best. The gull had run to the top half of the clover field and in due course it settled again in a nest of buttercups.

'If it can run as fast as that,' I said, 'it might escape a fox.'

'What about the second gull,' asked Jeannie, 'I mean the one you saw, and the one I saw in the lane?'

Rain from the south, seawards, had begun to spatter, a few drops heralding a downpour.

'Perhaps tomorrow will provide an answer,' I said.

It didn't. Soon after daybreak I got up and went to the bridge and looked across the valley. There was no white spot among the buttercups. No sign of a gull. We never saw a running gull again.

In this period of the year we used to have three thousand tomato plants in our greenhouses to look after. The variety we grew was called Maascross. We did not ourselves grow them from seed. We bought plants, specially grown for us to be ready by the middle of March by a nurseryman at Truro called Hitchens. These tomatoes had a very special flavour, a true tomato, and we had cards printed which read GROWN FOR FLAVOUR, and we pinned a card to each chip of tomatoes we took to our wholesaler. Some experts said that the flavour was due to the well water with which we watered them. Anyhow, our tomatoes gained a reputation and people asked specially for Tangye tomatoes. They still do . . . but now instead of three thousand tomato plants, we only grow a hundred. The reason is a conventional one. Three thousand plants require paid labour which cancels out any profit. A hundred plants we can manage on our own. There are, however, problems.

Our small reservoir, for instance, has silted up and we can no longer pump water to the greenhouses. This reservoir was dug by hand several years ago and caught the stream running from Monty's Leap to the sea. A mechanical digger, one might think, could be organised to dig out the silt, and this thought would be quite correct. Unfortunately such a mechanical digger would not be able to reach the reservoir without vandalising the surrounding land. Practical people would not mind this because they would value efficiency as the priority. Up to now Jeannie and I have not shared this view.

Hence we have had to find other ways to water the tomato plants and other crops we grow in the greenhouses; and we have found a way which, though not nearly as speedy as pumped water, serves the purpose.

We used our second well, the well in the lane which used to serve the farm at the top and by which we fill our home tank during the summer when our normal well is low. The water from this second well travels by gravity, needing no pumping, and at the point where the pipe nears the greenhouses I have a tap, and fastened to the tap is a half-inch polythene pipe which is connected to a watering system called 'Roots'. The system consists of half-inch polythene tubing, one hundred feet long or any other length you require. This is called a distribution tube and in it you punch nail-size holes at intervals of your own choosing, then insert into each hole a feeder tube about six inches long. The distribution tubing is attached to a valve unit which controls the flow of water, and there can be as many as four distribution tubings to one valve.

In this way I now water the tomato plants. I switch on the tap and the feeder tubes begin their drip, drip, drip, and I can go away, knowing the watering is being done for me. I use it also on other crops, inside' and outside the greenhouses, and because the tubing is flexible I can drape it around the garden in dry periods. It is, however, for produce that I must use it. Thus a row of peas will have a session, a row of onions, a row of runner beans.

Runner beans are considered to be difficult to grow in a greenhouse because the only point of growing them is to plant them early and so catch the high price of an early crop. But there is a snag. If it is a cold May bees do not come out of their hibernation and so, although the beans are in flower, the bees are not there to pollinate them. Hence the crop is sterile. Hence, if you ask an expert, they will tell you not to grow beans in a greenhouse.

Jeannie and I, however, were given a tip by an old gardener that if we grew sweet peas alongside the beans even the laziest most sleepy bee would be tempted to come out of hibernation, then proceed to do its duty on the runner bean flowers. So we grew sweet peas and for two years running we had a splendid crop of early runner beans. They fetched 60p a pound.

This year we became over-confident. We had done so well that we decided to expand the runner beans sowing and instead of having them in the Orlyt greenhouse in front of the cottage with the sweet peas growing beside them, we also sowed two rows in the other half of the greenhouse where we have our tomato plants. Tomato flowers, I said to Jeannie, would be to the runner beans what the sweet peas would be to the runner beans in the Orlyt. Lazy, sleepy bees would come out of hibernation for both groups of runner beans.

They didn't. True it was a cold May, especially early on, and a bee, even in the Orlyt, was so rare that when one of us saw one we rushed to the other, exclaiming: 'I saw a bee!' These rare bee appearances, however, achieved, all what we expected in the Orlyt. Excitedly, we watched the first flowers shed their petals and show the tiny green millimetre which would in due course grow into a succulent bean. The Orlyt, therefore, as in previous years, had fulfilled runner bean expectation.

Not so in the other greenhouse. Despite the cold weather the tomato plants, planted at the end of March, had produced their cluster of flowers on the first truss. We were pleased with them, although we were aware from past experience that if the cold weather persisted, especially cold nights, we would only have pimple-sized tomatoes on the first truss. None the less, the flowers were on the tomatoes and the flowers were on the runner beans. But nowhere in that greenhouse did I see a bee ... and the petals of the runner bean flowers began to fall without leaving any green millimetre behind them.

'We'll have to do something drastic,' I said to Jeannie.

I was particularly concerned because I had told our wholesaler that we would be having a bumper crop of runner beans, and I had described to him enthusiastically about the two long rows crowded with pink flowers (the variety was called Sunset) and he had replied: 'You'll make a lot of money.'

'Something drastic,' I repeated, 'what do you suggest, Jeannie?'

I had hoped she would take me seriously, but she didn't.

'Only one thing we can do,' she said laughing, 'and that is to catch an Orlyt bee and transport it!'

I laughed too.

'Right,' I said, 'we'll go bee-hunting.'

The sweet peas we grew were the old-fashioned scented variety. I had planted the seeds in pots during the winter and transplanted them into the Orlyt at the beginning of February. Sweet peas always remind me of that war film *Mrs Miniver*. There is a scene in that film when Mrs Miniver, who was played by Greer Garson, goes out into the garden one day during that frightening summer of 1940 and quietly goes round picking a basket of sweet peas. The scene has always remained in my memory for it was in such contrast to the battle that was taking place in the skies over England at that time.

'We can each take a handkerchief,' said Jeannie, 'and when we see a bee settle on a sweet pea we'll drop the handkerchief over it.'

The trouble was that even in the Orlyt the bees were still scarce. Only half a dozen or so had emerged from their hibernation and had been rewarded by sweet pea nectar. So it was a case of looking for one, then pouncing.

'I've got one!' Jeannie called out.

She gently folded the handkerchief over it, then we both hurried up to the tomato house, walked between the two rows of runner beans and, halfway, she opened the handkerchief and dropped the bee on an inviting pink flower.

We watched hopefully. Too hopefully.

For the bee promptly took off, buzzed a few yards in one direction, then another, and proceeded to settle, of all places, on the tiny white petals of the wretched *oxalis* which pester the ground in the greenhouse.

We caught other bees. They too treated the runner beans with disdain. Not until June did an armada of willing bees arrive in the greenhouse, and then it was too late. The price for runner beans had dived.

SIX

There was another problem besides the runner bean one in the greenhouse. A month after we planted the four rows of tomato plants, I forgot to close the sliding door one evening and the following morning I found a rabbit hole under one plant. The plant was in pieces, and so were a couple of others which the rabbit had hacked with its burrowing feet.

I was casual in my reaction. I said to myself that as I had left the door open I could expect a rabbit to have entered, and so I did nothing more than curse a little and fill in the hole that had been made. In any case an incident like this had happened before.

That night I carefully closed the sliding door, but the following morning the hole was there again.

Rabbits, pretty little rabbits with their endearing fictionalised ways, have captured the hearts of those who live in cement centres and close to the reliability of supermarket supplies. Those who grow the supplies, however, have a different attitude. Rabbits eat their livelihood. Rabbits multiply at such speed that while one year a row of carrots might be nibbled, the following year they are devoured.

In my case, I have in fact a large element of the cement-centre attitude. Rabbits are captivating to watch and they represent a sentimental form of freedom: a home in a burrow, a field in which to roam, scampers in the grass. But I have not always felt this way: long ago I used to shoot them and I enjoyed rabbit pie and rabbit stew, but never any more. The horrors of myxomatosis stopped that. Nor can I tolerate snares being used. Snares are as cruel as the gintrap, and they capture wandering cats as well. I prefer to leave the culling of the rabbit populations to nature; and this means leaving it to foxes, stoats and badgers which dig out rabbit nests . . . and to Ambrose. Ambrose in spring and summer is a great culler of rabbits. He will jump with his captive through the bedroom window at dead of night, carry it to the sitting-room, passing within twelve inches of my head on the pillow, and gorge his capture, leaving me to collect the remains first thing in the morning before Jeannie sees them.

Rabbits, as I have said, have been in the greenhouses before. On this particular occasion, however, I was faced with a situation which challenged my attitude towards growing. Was I still a professional grower of tomatoes, however small, or was I just growing for amusement? Whichever was the case tomato growing took a lot of our time during the course of the summer, so how could I allow a rabbit to dig up the plants and, I suspected, have its young in the hole it had made?

I had by now discovered a rabbit-sized tunnel under one side of the greenhouse (the greenhouse was originally a mobile so there was no brick base) and this I proceeded to block, and the rabbit proceeded to open. I was becoming impatient and this impatience one morning caused me to act in a way that was not my normal nature.

I was watering the plants by hose (this, of course, was before I discovered the Roots system), vacuously watching each plant receive its ration, then moving on to the next. I had gone up one row and reached the spot where instead of a plant the rabbit hole gaped at me, and then occurred the act which I quickly regretted. I turned the hose into the hole.

I only held it there for a few seconds . . . for suddenly to my horror there appeared peeping out of the hole, a baby

rabbit, water dripping from its whiskers, wide-eyed, bewildered. Naturally I swung the hose away. The baby rabbit continued to peer for a moment, then disappeared back underground.

The hole, I thought, could not have been flooded. Any other baby rabbits in there may have been dampened but they would be all right, and so from then on, as atonement for my thoughtless act, I let this rabbit family have the freedom of the greenhouse. I left the sliding doors open at night. The family could stay under glass when it was raining, go out in the open when it was fine, and, I am glad to say, no further damage was done.

I hope, however, it was not this family which decimated my Brussels sprouts plants a few weeks afterwards. The whole area was hemmed in by wire netting and yet the plants continued to be attacked. I presumed the rabbits jumped over the netting despite the fact it was three feet high, and though such a jump may sound unlikely, a Cornish cliff rabbit could do it without much difficulty. I have seen one. On the other hand, wood pigeons may have been the culprits. They certainly attack Brussels sprouts when they are well-established, savaging the sprouts with their beaks and tearing away the leaves. Never the less, it was rabbits I was blaming for the damage to my sprouts on that evening when a young German girl called Stephanie arrived at our door holding a cardboard box, saying: 'I've brought you a present!'

We had first met her a couple of years before when she was sixteen and on a camping holiday with three of her schoolfriends. They had camped nearby and in the morning they spent a while with us and Jeannie gave them breakfast. Afterwards Stephanie wrote us a letter of thanks, and an account of the rest of their camping holiday while walking on the coastal path round Cornwall. Thereafter she wrote from time to time, uninhibited in the telling of her hopes, enthusiasms and depressions.

I looked at the cardboard box. It was battered. There were several ragged holes in the lid.

'What *can* you have brought us?'

She was a slim girl, dark hair with a fringe wearing jeans and a loose blue shirt. She had arrived with a hiker's pack on her back and she had dumped this in the porch.

'I hope you will like them,' she said, and sounded hesitant. 'You see I was staying in a hostel in Exeter last night and I wanted to bring you a present, and then the daughter of the hostel owner told me she had these baby rabbits . . .'

'Rabbits?' I cried out.

'Yes,' said Stephanie, 'I knew how you love animals, and there were these two baby rabbits, and so we put them in a box and here they are.'

She handed the box to me.

'Jeannie,' I said, 'I don't dare look. You open it!'

Inside the box were the two baby rabbits, each about the size of a hand.

'But Stephanie,' said Jeannie, 'they're far too young to be separated from their mother.'

'And how did you travel with them, Stephanie? What train did you catch?' I asked.

'Oh no,' she said, 'I hitch-hiked. I started off from Exeter at seven this morning. I waited once for an hour but a car came along which took me to Penzance. Then another car took me to the end of your lane.'

I thought of her standing by the kerb, cardboard box beside her, two baby rabbits listening to the roar of the traffic.

'It was very kind of you to think of us,' I said, 'but ...'

I had been in the same situation myself. I have thought hard about giving a present to someone and when I gave it the present was a flop.

'You see,' I quietly explained, 'we have plenty of rabbits, and it just happens that this week they have demolished our brussels sprouts.'

'Oh dear,' she said, and I felt she might be close to tears, 'I've been so silly. I just didn't think,' and then she added: 'What can I do with them now?'

That was also troubling Jeannie and me.

It was getting late.

'Margaret,' said Jeannie suddenly. 'Margaret is the person who will help. She's got a tame rabbit!'

Margaret who helps us during the daffodil season. Margaret who with her husband George creates beautiful pottery at the end of our lane.

'Genius!' I said to Jeannie.

I thereupon collected the cardboard box and went down to the car, Stephanie following me, and off we went up the lane to Margaret. It was a silent journey, Stephanie whose English was unbelievably good, had nothing to say. She had had a long day. It had been a disaster.

It did not, however, end that way. Margaret took charge as soon as I had explained the situation, said she would look after the two rabbits overnight and that she would also telephone two mutual friends, in the area on holiday, who happened to love tame rabbits. The two mutual friends were both musicians. Malcolm Sutton, then eighteen years old, had walked down our winding lane soon after my book *A Gull on the Roof* was published and had come to see us regularly ever since. Ruth, whom he had recently married, is becoming a concert pianist of renown and she is also a tame-rabbit lover. She instantly agreed to accept the two rabbits and take them back to near Chester where they lived.

But one rabbit died during the night, despite Margaret's care. The other drove back to Chester with Ruth and Malcolm, and it thrived. They called it Smokey. So ends the story which began when a pretty German girl student hitch-hiked to Minack with a gift.

In late spring we were woken at daybreak on fine mornings by the descendants of Hubert the gull. Hubert was the first gull we ever saw perched on the cottage roof and the sight of him was of great significance to us at the time. We had that day experienced the total failure of our early potato crop, and we were broke, and the threat lay over us that we might have to return to the life in London from which we had escaped. Then suddenly we saw this gull on the roof. It seemed, at such a moment of emotion, that he had a message for us. We had been accepted by the mystical elements that pervade the Cornish cliffs. Our endeavours were seen to be real. We were not just flirting with Cornwall. Hubert the gull, though it may sound absurd to say so, changed our lives at that moment. We were no longer despondent. We became determined to survive.

Hubert was shot a while later by a young man with an airgun who used to roam the cliffs shooting at gulls. On the day it happened Hubert arrived at the cottage with a leg dangling and blood on a webbed foot. He circled the cottage but could not land, and when we threw him a piece of his favourite homemade bread, he hovered about it but could not reach it. We never saw him again after that day.

There have been other gulls. Gregory, a one-legged gull, Peter, Squeaker, Philip and Knocker; and there is now the evening gull who has no name but who just arrives when dusk is falling. There has also been, in the eyes of some visitors, a plastic gull on the roof. One of the gulls was roosting in stillness on the roof when a visitor called out: 'Look! They've got a plastic gull up there!'

It is difficult to be always correct when telling one gull from another. I am not sure, for instance, whether we still have the original Knocker and the original Philip. Gulls can live for twenty or thirty years and so there is every reason to believe they are the originals, for they certainly act in a similar way.

Knocker, for instance, still knocks on the glass roof of the porch. Frankly, it is a habit which infuriates us. When summer comes Jeannie is always trying to persuade me to shade the porch glass with a condiment which is supposed to remain all summer on the glass despite any rain. It is unfortunate that often when at last she has persuaded me to make the effort, the fixing of the ladder, the mixing of the condiment, the outstretched arm trying to reach the furthest point of the glass ... it is unfortunate how regularly a downpour will come, and wipe the glass clean.

However, Knocker does not operate in such devastating fashion. He destroys my shading gradually, using his webbed feet to do so. We will be sitting in the porch enjoying our breakfast and Knocker will plomp on the porch glass, and beat it with his beak. Or we will be indoors and hear this knock, knock, and will think the knock is that of a visitor. There have also been times when we have ignored this knock believing it was Knocker, then having to say to the visitor: 'We *are* sorry, we thought it was a gull.'

Knocker thus creates a problem in two ways: his webbed feet gradually clear the shading from the glass, so causing Jeannie again to persuade me to shade it; and with his knock which sounds like someone hitting thick glass with a mallet, he is threatening to break up the porch. So we shout at him and clap our hands: 'Go away, Knocker! Go away!'

Philip, meanwhile, has his quarters for most of the time on the cedarwood slated roof of the shelter where the tractor is kept just below the cottage. Or he will roost, as if on a nest, on the flat granite slab which protrudes from the rock foundations of the cottage, and where in time gone by they used to grind the family corn. This slab is close to our bedroom window and thus when Philip arrives at daybreak, the noise he makes wakes us up.

Not only the noise of Philip. Knocker will probably be performing his bashing on the porch, and junior gulls, offspring of the Knocker and Philip families, will also join in the screaming cacophony. They are shouting, presumably: 'Get up! Get up! We want our breakfast!' At such moments we dislike gulls. At such moments I yell at them and they will be silent for a second, then off they start screaming again.

Knocker and Philip never allow the junior gulls to stay for long, and though an occasional one will return to the cottage during the course of the day, it is Knocker and Philip who alone proceed to dominate us. It seems absurd that a gull can dominate a human being but it is so. The late Lord St Levan, whose home was the castle St Michael's Mount, used to wear an old felt hat as he wandered around his grounds. A gull in the neighbourhood took a fancy to this hat and week after week, month after month, whenever Lord St Levan went for his walk, the gull appeared and dived upon him. Eventually the gull was trapped and transported to Somerset where it was let free – and perhaps set off to find another gentleman wearing an old felt hat.

The domination of Knocker and Philip over us is not so eccentric. It only concerns food, and their tactics vary according to the urgency of their appetites. If it is on a small-snack level, they will follow us with their beady eyes as we walk by, sometimes muttering muted gull noises but never getting up from their roosting spot. If, however, their appetites are on a main-course level they will stand up, stamp up and down, swoop their beaks towards the sky and let out a cascade of gull screams. Such a moment is when we are dominated.

'Have you something for the gulls?' I will call out urgently to Jeannie.

'I fed them an hour ago.'

'They want more!'

'Tell them', Jeannie has sometimes replied defiantly, 'there's plenty of fish in the sea!'

Those who pander to their pets, whether they are dogs, cats, budgerigars or hamsters, are anathema to those who cannot relate to animals. Profound psychological reasons are said to be the cause of our behaviour: lack of love in childhood; lack of parenthood; lack of a direction in our lives. Yet all we want to do is give love without complication.

Knocker and Philip, or their occasional companions, are not, of course pets. They are far too independent. It just happens that they chose to adopt us and make use of us, and in return we oblige them because we remember the sight of the first gull on the roof and are sentimental about the connection. Thus these gulls continue daily to fly up the valley from the sea, and it is only when there is a raging storm that we do not see them. Then we wait for them. We wait because we have learnt from experience that they will return when the storm is ending. 'The gulls are back,' I will call to Jeannie, 'the storm will soon be over.' And it is.

We had other bird problems that late spring. There was the annual one of the magpie nests: where were they? when should I remove the eggs?

I do not like magpies. I admire their smart black and white plumage and their general jauntiness as they hop about a field, but their harsh, noisy chatter as they raid the nests of other birds, taking the eggs or the fledgelings, makes me determined to control their spread.

In March, I have regularly observed, the magpies of the district hold a meeting. I have no idea how extensive the district may be as far as the magpies are concerned, but every year upwards of sixteen magpies gather together on some corner of our land. I have seen them, for instance, on the top corner of the clover field, some on the ground, some perched among the bare tops of the blackthorn, some on the stone hedge, and they have remained there for most of the day, endlessly chattering, bouncing their long tails up and down. Another year I have seen this behaviour repeated in a corner of the QE2 field, and on these occasions it is obvious that a very important conference is in progress. Is the purpose to arrange marriages between the young of the previous year? (Magpies mate for life.) Or is it to discuss housing arrangements, the allocation of nestsites, thus ensuring that there are never too many magpie fledgelings competing for too few little bird fledgelings?

Soon I start to keep watch for the beginning of a magpie nest. I can, of course, only watch for those on our land, but as I usually find three this means that at least fifteen magpies will not be plundering the countryside if I reach the eggs before they are hatched. I will go out early in the morning, because that is when nest building is at it busiest, and I will scan the land with my fieldglasses. I look carefully in Minack wood because there is usually one there, and I keep a special watch on the dense blackthorn wherever it may be, but particularly where it crowds the cliff around our daffodil meadows.

This year I found the expected three nests by the middle of April and then I had to wait until I judged that all the eggs had been laid. The nest in the wood I tackled too soon for I found only two eggs, but their removal was enough to scare the magpies away. The second nest caused me some distress. A pair of magpies, a first-year bride and bridegroom I suspect, had foolishly proceeded to build a nest in the crabapple tree exactly opposite the barn. My distress was due to watching their doomed hard work, the bringing of sticks in their beaks, the ever-growing edifice, eventually capped by a dome of sticks with a side entrance which was aimed to defeat marauders. I watched them going to and fro, then waited during the silent period while the eggs were laid ... and then up with my ladder, a hand inside the nest, and I had the five mottled-blue eggs. I was distressed though. I had become too well acquainted with those two magpies whose family I had destroyed.

The third nest was situated in the centre of what appeared to be an impenetrable mass of blackthorn just below what we call the far meadows where the miniature *obvallaris* daffodil grows. The nest was at least thirty feet inside the mass of blackthorn and what was to happen to me in my attempt to reach it must have made the magpies say: 'Serves you right!'

Clambering through blackthorn tears trousers and shirts, cuts hands and bare arms. I struggled my way towards the nest, was at last within reach when suddenly found myself falling. Intent on forcing my way through the blackthorn I had failed to realise that my feet were on a ridge of blue elvin. The ridge had come to its end, and I fell. The fall was only about five feet, but when I picked myself up I realised there was something wrong with my leg, and I was to find that I had torn a ligament which meant visits to our local osteopath before it healed. Did I, however, collect the eggs I had made such an effort to reach? The effort had been made too late. The eggs had hatched. The magpies had won.

There were other nests to observe. There was that of the mistle thrush, the Storm Cock of the winter who from a bare branch will hurl its melodious song into the Cornish gales. At nesting-time the bird is silent except for the churring sound it makes when it believes a threat exists. It often made a churring sound this spring because the siting of the nest was unwise. It was in the fork of an *olearia*, a windbreak tree which comes from New Zealand, just a bunch of sticks, and it was close to the coastal path. One of the mistle thrushes would perch on a hawthorn not far away, very still for twenty minutes or more, keeping watch; and then someone would come up the coastal path and the churring, like a rattle, would begin. No harm came to this mistle thrush family. No human being disturbed them, no magpie, no crow. It was pleasing, having watched from the beginning, to see the parents and the three young feeding one day in the grass of the stable field. For the nest had seemed so vulnerable.

A pair of green woodpeckers were nesting in the wood. They chose to bore their hole in an elm that is on the edge of the meadow where we grow Joseph McLeod daffodils which, for some peculiar reason, will rarely flower, though in other meadows they flower profusely. It was an elm which was so far untouched by elm disease. Many elms around Minack have died, but when we cut them down we do not go to ground level. We leave a trunk around six feet high which becomes covered with ivy and helps to soften the loss of the trees. We also have a remarkable number of elm saplings growing up, and indeed they sometimes cause me inconvenience. They are growing merrily, for instance, in our small orchard, peering up through the apple tree branches and those of the pears, and some have grown taller than the cherry trees. In normal circumstances I could cut them down. But how can I do so when the elm tree is a rarity?

Woodpeckers are also victims of elm disease: ornithologists are wondering how they are going to adapt to the changed environment. We see only green woodpeckers in this area of Cornwall and they have come to Minack over the years. Their call is like somebody laughing and it echoes on sunlit days, a wild uninhibited cry of joy. When one looks whence it comes, one perhaps will see a flash of green, and the evanescent red of the head as it hammers with its beak into the trunk of a tree. Once upon a time I believed that whenever I heard the tattoo of a woodpecker beak, it was intent on making the hole which was to become its nest. True this sometimes is the reason, but more often it is drilling a hole to get at the insects which live within the tree. They are great insect-eaters, and ant-eaters. I have often, on early summer mornings, seen a woodpecker digging at an ant heap which I had only discovered the day before.

Woodpeckers may, however, be yet another endangered species of wildlife. In this case it is not the fault of the human race but of nature. The human race in its daily slaughter of trees for commercial purposes, may play a part. Indeed if elm trees had been of commercial value they would largely have been destroyed over the years, but they were not of commercial value and so in this case one cannot blame the human race. Nature is responsible, and so one wonders for what reason Creation has decided upon a worldwide change.

For woodpeckers there is a temporary advantage. Decaying elms may result in vanishing sites, but for the time being they provide the woodpeckers with a gourmet menu of insects.

As for our personal woodpeckers, there was to be no trouble for them. One year such a woodpecker family, nesting near to the cottage, had its eldest fledgling killed by a carrion crow on its first flight. We saw it happen. On this occasion, however, soon after I had observed the green woodpeckers had made their hole and their nest in the elm, I also observed a carrion crow's nest high up in a tree nearby and I was able to bash the nest down before the eggs had been hatched. No torn ligament this time.

There were, of course, the nests of our resident small birds, like the dunnocks, the blackbirds who in early summer keenly await the ripening of the tomatoes, and Charlie and Shelagh the chaffinches. Successive chaffinches have been called Charlie and Shelagh. The first Charlie became a strange mourner for a cat. He adopted us a couple of years before Monty died, hopping about the garden, piping his note, demanding food and showing no fear whatever of Monty. Monty himself had never shown interest in catching birds, though I was always aware that it would be natural for him to pounce if they came too close to him. Charlie used to come close to him, but Monty would only sleepily look at him, and so what happened on the day that Monty died is perhaps understandable. Jeannie had laid him on lush green grass just outside the cottage. The sun was shining, warming him, and on a rock a few feet away was Charlie, quite still.

Thus tame male chaffinches are called Charlie, three generations of them since the original one, and the lady chaffinches are called Shelagh after the shy, teenage girl who once worked for us. One day Shelagh said to Jeannie that she thought the dim-coloured lady chaffinch had one of the sweetest faces of any little bird she had seen. The remark stayed with Jeannie's memory and so the lady chaffinches are called Shelagh as a kind of memorial.

It is convenient to give names to birds which haunt the neighbourhood of one's home. It is a practical act, as practical as being able to look out of one's window and say: 'Mrs Smith is walking down the street.' Thus another bird who was given a name by Jeannie was a wood pigeon she decided to call Peggy.

Peggy chose, of all places, to build her nest in Annie's Folly. Here was the *macrocarpa* – which I had planted in the belief that it was a scented mediterranean heather, and instead may grow to 100 feet high – now adding to my dislike of it by housing the nest of a wood pigeon.

'If you feel as you do about wood pigeons,' said Jeannie calmly, 'all you have to do is treat Peggy like you have done the magpies and the carrion crows.'

Peggy ... the name identified her as someone special. I did not think of her in the category of a nameless magpie or a nameless carrion crow. There was personality in Peggy. Peggy, however, was now to have her own problems. It was a still period of weather when she made her nest of a few sticks. Then the gales came, and we watched the *macrocarpa* swaying, the branches jumping, and all the while Peggy sitting on her nest, holding tight, like someone on a horror swing in a fun fair. I came to admire Peggy. But next year, no doubt, her offspring will eat our sprouts.

There was another nest this spring which never materialised; and this was due to Mingoose Merlin.

Up to two years before, swallows nested either in the stable or the so-called garage, and I always presumed they belonged to the same family. Then one autumn there was severe weather in the mediterranean while the autumn migration was taking place, and there was a consequent huge loss of life among the swallows. No swallow appeared with us the following year. No swallow the year after that. We presumed that family had been lost.

This year a pair did appear and began to create their mud-built nest up against a rafter in the stables, the stables where the donkeys receive mince pies on Christmas Eve and where in summer they like to shelter, away from the heat and the flies.

The swallows had completed their nests when a heatwave began and the donkeys proceeded to stay in the stables rather than outside.

The entrance to the stables is door-sized. Mingoose

Merlin liked to fill it, bottom to the dark inside, head to the fresh air.

The swallows, however, objected.

They deserted their mud-built nest.

SEVEN

On early summer mornings the scent of dew-touched honeysuckle breathes across our land, reminding me of the *tiare tahiti*, the flower of the South Seas, the flower the girls of Tahiti used to garland their lovers and now garland tourists.

I was there during the years before the Hitler war, lured there because it was a romantic world loved by Gauguin, Somerset Maughan, Robert Keable and Rupert Brooke, and all who sought tranquillity and happiness away from the conventions of western civilisation.

I have a tangible memento of my time there: a *pareu*. A *pareu* is about five feet long and three feet wide and the cloth of mine has variegated patterns in red and yellow. I had many uses for it in the South Seas. Sometimes I used it as a carrier bag, wrapping my belongings in it, tying it on the handlebars of my bicycle when I pedalled round Tahiti or Moorea. Sometimes I used it as a sheet to cover me on hot steamy nights and often I used it as a towel after a swim in a lagoon.

The main purpose, of course, is to wear it, either by wrapping it round your middle like a bath towel, or in the more complicated way of the local inhabitants. This latter way can cause predicaments unless tied correctly. I had such a predicament one night when I was energetically dancing at a birthday party where I was the only European present. I was staying at the time in a *faré* built on bamboo sticks at Papeari at the far end of Tahiti, and my host was a fat, happy old Tahitian called Mauu, a legendary figure in the islands, who had known my heroes like Gauguin and Rupert Brooke. There I was dancing when my *pareu* slipped. Everyone roared with laughter and Mauu called out in Tahitian, and by this time I spoke the language: 'You're in good company: Rupert Brooke was the same, he could never keep his *pareu* up either!'

It was an eerie moment in my life: a guitar playing, dancers stamping their feet, a lilting sound of singing, water lapping bamboo stilts, a moon shining above the Presqu' Isle de Tahiti . . . and suddenly I was linked with a man who wrote:

> *Manua, when our laughter ends,*
> *And hearts and bodies, brown as white,*
> *Are dust about the doors of friends*
> *Or scent ablowing down the night,*
> *Then oh! then, the wise agree,*
> *Comes our immortality.*

Lines too simple for many, but from a schoolboy they had captured me . . . a poignant cry about transient love.

I was emotionally ready, therefore, when I went to the South Seas. I had already experienced some ego trip success in that I had been a columnist on a national newspaper, and seen my photograph on London buses, and I had already done enough to tire of the tinsel of it. When I went to the South Seas I was already on my way, unsuspecting, to Minack. For when at last I had to leave those lovely islands where I felt so free, where I was a traveller, not a tourist on a package tour, not a media man with a film unit, where I became aware that one can live unselfconsciously, that inward enlightenment only comes with solitude . . . I made a vow that when I returned to western civilisation I would set out to find a reflection of my South Sea Islands' happiness.

One early honeysuckle-scented morning I decided to read again my South Seas diary and I took the bound volume, pages filled with the scrawl of my writing, to the homemade seat in the meadow by Honeysuckle Corner. I read again the haphazard comments, the instant impressions which were to lead me to Minack:

December 5th

I woke when it was still dark after but one hour's sleep. The yobo-type Americans (I was travelling steerage from Panama) had become the previous evening more rowdy than ever. Wanting to get away from them I lugged my mattress up through the hatch and settled down, but I had left my watch behind and went back to fetch it. When the Americans saw me they gave me a cheer and dived at me, shouting: 'Let's push him back naked!'

Needless to say I didn't appreciate their form of humour, and at first I struggled politely despite there being five of them. When, however, they started to manhandle me, I began to hit out more wildly than I have ever done before in my life.

I slithered myself free from one who was trying to hold my arms, plunged my left hand repeatedly at another, and succeeded in making a rabbit punch on a third. It wasn't long before they scattered, and then I was amazed to hear one of them say: 'Damned unsporting of you to hit out like that!' Dear me, dear me, I never want to see my travelling companions again.

But, as I said, it was still dark when I woke up and I had that feeling which one always has when one knows something exciting or unusual is going to happen: a kind of tightness in the head. And as I rubbed my eyes I suddenly saw, as if only a few yards away, a huge blackness even blacker than the night. Slowly we were passing it and, each minute, more of this blackness came into view.

100

I left my mattress quickly and, only faintly feeling the bruises of the night before, I hurried to the hold to collect my belongings. Then I went again on deck and ran along to the bows where only the silent Swede, motionless as usual, was sitting.

The darkness had turned into grey and within a few minutes as I stood there, the grey turning to yellow, I saw in the east the golden rays of the coming sun.

We were going at half speed, cutting through the water as we would have done a river with no current, or as if we were sailing through a giant millpond. Just a cool swish.

But the sun was edging upwards from the horizon, and the sky and the thin clouds were turning into blues and pinks, mauves and yellow. The land which was Tahiti was transforming from its darkness, and each minute I saw more of its foliage, more of the valleys, more of the jagged mountaintops.

I stood there in the bow feeling the South Seas were not disappointing me, and that I would find the peace the rest of the world despised.

And as I was thinking this, two things happened: first the sun shot the sky into blazing gold; and then as I was marvelling, a beautiful scent softened the air, the scent of the *hibiscus* and of the *tiare tahiti*.

I was moved as I have never been moved. Every emotion crowded into my body and I wanted to shout, and cry, and laugh. I stood there murmuring incoherently, and laughing, and gripping the handrails of the deck. It was too wonderful a moment to last. The Swede and I were no longer alone. One of the Americans had joined us.

December 11th

I have been a week here and I am staying at the Hotel Tahiti, kept by a one-time defrocked French priest so people describe the proprietor; and I am in a large, scrupulously clean room with a balcony as big as any room; and it faces the street and the lagoon on the other side of the street.

I am sitting there now watching the world go by. There are half a dozen sailing boats tied up on the other side of the street and in the hazy distance I see the island of Moorea, and away to the west the sun is beginning to set.

Everything is so clean. The girls passing below me are in tiny white shorts and blouses made of the material of the *pareu*, in red and greens and orange. Their jet-black hair falls down their backs, combed and brushed so that it gleams; and their skin is golden-brown. Sometimes they wear sandals, sometimes they are bicycling barefoot. They never wear hats, just a flower stuck behind their ears: behind the left ear, I have just learnt, if they are looking for a lover, behind the right ear if they are temporarily committed.

By Western standards their behaviour is hopelessly immoral. A sex affair to them has the same fun as a game of tennis, and no more importance. Laborie, a retired French diplomat whom I have made friends with and who has lived here many years, says a European will go mad if he falls in love with a Tahitian girl. She will always be unfaithful to him for she doesn't take sex seriously. She treats it as a delightful entertainment. I have also met a disillusioned white Russian called Paul who has been here ten years: 'It's all a joke in this goddam country, nothing is serious.'

December 16th

I've been suffering from depression. It is absurd that I should have felt like this because I am in the place I have always wanted to be, but I miss being in touch with my family. And I've been having too much rum, too many late nights, and not living the kind of life I dreamt about. And so I've crossed the water to this lovely island of Moorea, and I feel happy again.

102

I've been having a fascinating time and met two characters which seem straight out of Maugham's *The Moon and Sixpence*. One is the proprietor of the hotel at Afareitu where I've been staying. He is a Swiss called Heuberger, about forty years old, who used to manage one of the top hotels of St Moritz, and who was married, he told me, to the daughter of the owner of the best-known hotel on the French Riviera. He became fed up pandering to the rich and famous and became obsessed by the idea of doing a Gauguin, cutting himself off completely from the life in which he had for so long been immersed. He walked out on his wife and sailed for Tahiti. His life today is such a contrast. He has married the Tahitian schoolmistress of the village, and that means he embraces all her family. Yet he still retained the suave manner of a sophisticated hotel manager, greeting me when I arrived as if I was a very important guest. He didn't speak much about his life, but I will always remember his answer to my question as to whether he would ever return to his old life. 'I'll never cross the ocean again,' he said, 'I have found peace. Here will I die.'

What is this sad look that native girls have in their eyes? And why have all their songs got pathos in their notes? They show no sadness in their way of living.

After Heuberger I met this Englishman who looked like a retired Camberley Colonel, except that he was wearing a *pareu* instead of a suit and was living with a native girl, and had a cow in the garden. He thought the world was mad with which, of course, I agreed. He talked about how the Americans were burning wheat because they had too much while a few hundred miles away people were starving, and how surplus coffee was being thrown away while millions couldn't afford to buy it. Then on he went about the world being full of untold riches of coal and yet people shivered in their houses. About nations he said only the few manipulated the conditions for war. For all these troubles he blamed the intellectuals. Those, he said, who topped the examinations lists in universities all over the world, and who are so clever, so confident in believing they are the elite, that they have no time for common sense.

I was impressed by him. Then he talked about Hitler ranting at the German people about war and scaring the rest of us. And he denounced the foreign offices of the world who had let him reach this stage. Strangely enough, and I am not exaggerating, the world from here does seem to me to be mad! I was only with him for an hour or two, but I will always remember him, and also his last words to me: 'There will always be rivalry and bitterness between nations. From this spot where we are now I see the world as if it were a glass bowl and inside the fishes are swimming round and round, without end and without meaning.' It was useful to listen to him. It jerked me out of complacency, reminded me how lucky I was to be in the South Seas.

January 7th

I came upon a wedding feast on the day I left Moorea to come back to Papeete. It had already lasted three days and there were another three days to go. At the head of the table sat the bridegroom, his head cupped sadly in his hands, and beside him was his bride, her hair hanging in straggles over a tired, pinched face.

January 10th

A most extraordinary thing happened today. Quite unbelievable. When I arrived at Panama before taking the *Villa d'Amiens* for Tahiti, I found to my horror that my money had disappeared from my suitcase, consisting of a twenty-dollar bill, two ten-dollar and a five. Not a sign of them anywhere, and not a sign of them since although I have used the suitcase every day, using it as a sort of wardrobe. This morning I went to it and there bang on top of my clothes were all the dollar bills that had gone missing! How can it be explained? Of course, I am wildly excited and have decided to leave Tahiti and go and explore the magical islands of Raiatea, Tahaa, Huahine, and Bora Bora. They are called Les Isles sous le Vent.

January 16th

The boat I was due to sail on, called the *Poti Raiatea*, that looks like a battered and ancient Scottish trawler, has engine trouble, and I didn't go yesterday. Instead I went out to Papeari and saw Mauu again . . . and nearly lost my life! What happened was that I borrowed an outrigger canoe and started to paddle across the lagoon to a small island I had fallen in love with on my first visit, even had a fantasy of building a house there. But I hadn't reckoned that a breeze would suddenly turn into a strong wind when I was halfway across. Suddenly little waves began to splash into the canoe, and it got fuller and fuller till I found it was waterlogged, and my paddling oar was useless. I had half a coconut in the canoe and I tried to bale out the water, then I began to yell, and was in a panic. Then I found myself in the lagoon holding on to the canoe and treadmilling with my legs. But as I did so I had to let go of my oar and in an attempt to reach it I let go of the coconut, and so there I was alone and without foreseeable help.

In one direction two hundred yards away was the shore, but there was a strong current against me if I tried to swim there. The other shore was five hundred yards away and I began to half swim, half push the swamped canoe in that direction for I thought the canoe would give me a base as I grew tired. The worst moment was to come. I suddenly remembered the *barracouda*, the killer shark-type creature which had torn the leg off a swimmer a short time before . . .

and then I saw two huge birds circling above me and my imagination made me believe they were vultures. I was now swimming on my back and had left the canoe, and I thought how foolish to end my life in this way. I felt tireder and tireder, and no longer worried about the *barracouda* . . . and suddenly my head hit something. An iron post. I had reached shore.

January 24th

I sailed from Papeete in the *Poti Raiatea* three days ago. We left in the evening, a swarm of locals on the deck, and there were babies, and one screamed all night. I had a couchette just above the oil-smelling engine, and beside me a Tahitian couple with two children, and as my sleepless night wore on they offered me a bamboo to eat. It was a quiet crossing though the boat seemed dangerously overloaded, and I was fearful that a breeze might suddenly blow up. In the early hours the engine broke down and we drifted for an hour or so before they got it going. There were many on the quay to see us off. We should have gone at five but there was some trouble with the rudder and we didn't leave till seven. But those seeing us off waited patiently as if time did not matter. Men standing on the quay, hand on their bicycles, women in bright dresses waving handkerchiefs, groups of girls chattering, hauntingly beautiful with their long black hair, a *tiare tahiti* or a scarlet hibiscus behind an ear. On the *Poti Raiatea* as she moved away from the quay, a man with a guitar began singing *Hoi Mai* and everybody joined in. A Tahitian beside me said: 'Un joli départ.'

We called first at the island of Tahaa, then after a short stop we went on to Raiatea and tied up alongside the ramshackle pier of Utora, its main village. Not pretty. Just one street with ugly corrugated-iron red roofs. I took a room in the so-called hotel, kept by a voluble little Italian called Fontana who seems rather nice. Anyhow he did me a service by introducing me to Gouwe, and I had dinner with him. He is an elderly Dutch painter whose work I had seen in Papeete and admired. He is another escapist from Western civilisation. There are so many of them. Just before I left Papeete I met Alain Gerbault, the legendary French lone sailor. He was sitting on a bench beside the Papeete lagoon, barefoot, wearing a *pareu*, thumbing through a London yachting magazine: 'I am looking to see what I shall give myself for a present: that clock with a ship's bell or that knife with a cork handle which never sinks?' He told me of a friend of his in Bora Bora with whom I could stay, and I am now waiting for a fishing boat to take me to Bora Bora.

After I had dinner with Gouwe he asked me if I would like to see the wild part of the island where he lived. He said he only came to Utora to get drunk. I said I would go with him and next day we set out in a launch, Fontana coming with us, and a man called Paul Nordman, another escapist from the Western civilisation who found only a few years ago a small wooden statue created by Gauguin. We arrived at Gouwe's house after an hour and I was left there with Gouwe while the other two sailed on round the island on some business of their own.

Gouwe's house, or *faré*, is in a superb bay all by itself. It leans into the lagoon and water laps under the verandah. There was a large room and a small one, with bamboo walls, and strewn around were his canvases. I had brought with me four bottles of red wine and two tins of corn beef, and my belongings were wrapped as usual in one of my *pareus*. That evening he told me he became famous in Holland and Paris as a painter of horses, and he became tired always having to paint horses; so eleven years ago, in the manner of Gauguin, he disappeared, and came to the South Seas. He found Tahiti too civilised for him and so he came the two hundred miles to Raiatea, and built this *faré* over the lagoon. 'J'aime la solitude,' he said, adding that only in solitude can anyone find their true selves.

Much about him reminded me of the characters of Somerset Maughan. About women he said there was happiness in the South Seas because no one had any conscience about having sex. Tensions, he said, had no need to build up. Girls had many lovers because it was natural. Europeans, he said, were humbugs when they condemned prostitutes or easily available women. Sex never did any harm. Tensions which built up, he said, could result in terrible harm. I thought of Sadie Thompson as he spoke.

He talked about his work and how he believed that he was a great painter but that he would only be recognised after his death. He was ill, I realised that. Around his lips was the brown nicotine from the cigarettes, drooping little things, which he rolled himself. There were red marks on his face, as if they were cuts, and his right eye was watery and half-closed. He talked a lot about 'mon grand tableau' and he showed it to me, two natives, branches of bananas on their shoulders pushing their way through undergrowth.

I was up early next morning and Gouwe was already working. Then I heard in the distance but coming closer and closer two children's voices singing in the hoarse attractive way of the native. 'Voilà notre café,' said Gouwe, 'don't show yourself and they will go on singing right into this room.'

I bought one of his small pictures although I had no francs to spare. It is a beautiful picture of a lagoon in brilliant colours and, who knows, I may find I have a Gauguin in years to come. Just as I left him to return to Utora, he mentioned the man and wife who looked after him and who live a mile away. He explained that the chicken we had had for dinner had been killed by them specially for me, and he asked me to go and thank them. 'They are sensitive people,' he said.

January 30th
I have found the South Sea Island of my dreams. I realise now that Papeete and the island of Tahiti, even Moorea, belong to the tourist traveller. I had too many hangovers, experienced too many of the situations which were echoes of my life in London and New York. But now...

I set sail for Bora Bora, forty miles away from Raiatea, in a sailing cutter called the *Teriori Nohori* at noon the day after I left Gouwe. There were two other passengers, Leon, a pearl merchant whose home was in Tahiti, and Lia, an American girl, a painter, who has been wandering the South Seas on her own for four months. The crew were four natives and there was also the wife of the skipper. She has a terrible case of *féfé*, or elephantisis. She lay below in a fever most of the time, but occasionally she heaved herself onto the deck, and in native fashion asked blunt questions in a simple way. 'Which one is your lover?' she asked Lia.

It was very hot and there was no breeze, and instead of being the usual five-hour voyage, we did not reach the pass into the lagoon of Bora Bora until midnight. The skipper was nervous of the currents, and so we anchored, and watched the stars, and Lia pointed out to me the three stars of Orion and the little group called the Pleiades, then added she would always think of this voyage whenever she saw them, wherever she might be.

In the morning we tied up at Vaitape and booked into the little hotel, and Leon jokingly told me not to take the best room overlooking the lagoon. 'Why?' I asked. 'There was a proprietor of this hotel who had leprosy. He lived in that room while his wife looked after the guests,' was his reply.

But I stayed in the hotel only two days because an island across the lagoon lured me and I borrowed a canoe and went there, and here I am. It is called Toopua. Toopua means branch of the Pua tree, and there is a legend that if you went to the island, found a branch and brought it back with you, you would draw the island to Bora Bora so that it joined. There are beaches of white sand and sudden bays and inlets, and deep, deep water so blue and clear that staring from a canoe into the depths you see another world of many-coloured fishes swimming lazily among a forest of luxuriant vegetation. It takes about an hour to walk round it, and at one point there is the little island of Tabu a hundred yards away. Long years ago a battle was fought there and history says that the loser put a curse on the little island, foretelling ill luck to anyone who stayed there, so declaring it Tabu. A few years ago Murnau, the German film director, made the film there called *Tabu*. First the negative of his picture was burnt and then a year or so later he was killed in a motor accident. Today it is just a little island overcome by vegetation.

Lia and Leon came with me to the island for a few days; and first Leon left, then Lia. I am glad they have gone. Leon had begun to tire me with his personal problems, and Lia was always too busy. Every minute had to be filled with activity so that the sense of timelessness did not exist when in her company. I felt I ought to have met her in Paris, or London, or New York. Not in the South Seas.

110

So now I am alone except for the young couple, the only occupants of the island with their two very young children, and a girl called Maeva, half-Chinese, half-Tahitian, who appeared on the island yesterday afternoon and shows no sign of leaving.

February 7th
Will I ever be so happy again? Can there be any place in the world which is so peaceful and beautiful? Last night I joined the fishermen searching for lobsters and crabs on the reef surrounding Bora Bora. The moon was full and it was like daylight as we searched, and yet it was not daylight, the light was ethereal. This morning Maeva asked me whether I would like a red fish or a black fish or a white fish with blue spots for breakfast. It seems a silly question but there are all these multicoloured fishes which are good to eat. I said I would like a red fish and she ran across the few yards of white sand and dived into the lagoon carrying a *patia*, a spear, in her right hand, and five minutes later she was back with two red fish. She disappeared for an hour later in the morning and when she returned she had a chain of *tiare tahiti* which she had expertly tied; and she put it round my shoulders, and I breathed its scent. She laughs and plays with the spirit of a child who knows no trouble, and yet there is at times a faraway look in her eyes, a sadness. Or perhaps what I see is a reflection of my own feelings. Spared the crudeness of Western civilisation, what has she and all those who live in the these islands got to fear? Their riches are around them: bananas and coconuts hang in clusters on the trees, fish in abundance, life without envy.

But I have to return to civilisation and all the stresses it brings. I am the one who is sad.

February 14th
For the rest of my life I will be looking for an island like that

of my island of Toopua. I am leaving within the next few days, and no doubt as I say goodbye I will promise that one day I will return, but I know in my heart that I never will. What would I do if I lived here? I am young and the years lie ahead of me, all the exciting adventures and failures and successes. I would tire of being a beachcomber. I've just been lucky to have had a dream that has been fulfilled, and I have learnt of some basic things I want from life. I want honesty from those I deal with. I want to find someone to bring out the better qualities in me. I want to find somewhere to live where there can be solitude. I want to be like the old Colonel of Moorea who viewed the world in detached fashion. I want to be free to make my own decisions and not be influenced by political groups. I want to wake up every morning knowing that I am an individual and not one of the herd. I said all this to Maeva this morning as we lay on the sand, and I spoke in English so she didn't understand a word. She just looked at me, then picked up a handful of sand and banged it down on my tummy. 'Mamu mata nehene,' she said, which meant 'shut up kind eyes', and then she added: 'Quelle bêtise tu parles!' (What nonsense you talk!). And I marvelled at her intuition, and thought of the lines of Rupert Brooke:

> There's wisdom in women, of more than they have known,
> And thoughts go blowing through them, are wiser than their own.

She is right. Once involved again in Western civilisation, I will forget my good intentions.

I did not, however, forget, and as a result I was sitting in Honeysuckle Corner with the scent of the honeysuckle pervading the soft, morning air just as the scent of the *tiare tahiti* pervaded the air of the South Seas. I had found my Toopua.

Jeannie, when I was in the South Seas, had also found her version of a South Sea Island which was to influence her always. Pinchaford was the name, an old farmhouse on the edge of Dartmoor where she remembers sun-drenched holidays, uninhibited happiness, early-morning gallops across the bracken-covered moors, lazing by the swimming pool, laughing with young men who were soon to die in the war.

Pinchaford was her Toopua. She too, unsuspectingly, was on her way to Minack.

Pinchaford

EIGHT

This summertime, on days when the sun burnt down on Minack and the nights were warm, Ambrose changed his habits and developed a midsummer madness. He no longer slept on our bed so leaving me free to turn when I wished to turn, and to stretch my legs, and be spared my foolish concern that I might be upsetting him.

Instead, as dusk fell, he set out on a prowl around his private world. He had many enquiries to make, many places to visit. There was the hole, a mere crack between two rocks, through which a mouse escaped from him on the previous night. There was another hole in the corner of the stables where the bracken of donkey winter bedding was stored which, he believed, housed a family of mice. Such holes had to be watched.

These, however, were mundane adventures of the night, routine tasks. It was when he set off up the lane that the real excitement of the night began. There were, in the stillness, so many unexplained rustles in the undergrowth on either side. Was it a frog, or a mole, or a mouse, or a nibbling rabbit? He was in no hurry to find out. He was not hungry. He had had a plate of coley for supper. He could enjoy the luxury of prolonging his excitement. A curious rustle... and he could sit and watch and wait. He was like an angler on a riverbank.

At his leisure he would move away, and sometimes, after crossing Monty's Leap he would turn left into the greenhouse field, where the California daffodils grow, and where, wired in, is the kitchen garden. If he is in the mood he will jump up on the post which holds the hinges of the gate and proceed to patrol the kitchen garden. He performs on these occasions a valuable task, because mice proliferate, coming as they do from the adjacent wood, and they steal the pea seeds I have planted, and the lettuce seeds. Thus, in his role of a security officer, I welcome Ambrose's visits to the kitchen garden.

Or he will stroll on up the lane, where there are threats at night which are not there in a stroll up the lane during the day. An owl may be watching him, squeaking angry noises in its belief that he is a hunting rival, and there are other roamers of the night, the occasional badger or fox. The further up the lane from the cottage, the more rabbits will be hopping about their business. There may also be a wandering cat to meet, a cat from the farm at the top where our friend Walter Grose, the Pied Piper of cats, has an assorted collection. Every moment is a potential thrill and he will position himself, half-hidden in a spread of couch grass and bracken at the side of the lane, and watch.

In the early hours he will return to the cottage, jump through the wide-open window, pass through the tiny bedroom and then through the sitting-room into the spare room where he will curl himself on a shirt that I have left on the bed. Strangely, above the bed hangs a painting by Jeannie of Monty, also curled up asleep. Later, much later, when he wakes up and thinks it time for his breakfast, he will come to us, jump on the bed and yap.

I do not, however, welcome these summer-night sorties. I always have at the back of my mind that a rogue fox might catch him, just as I always feared that a rogue fox might catch Lama or Oliver. After all a rogue fox *did* chase Monty. Monty hurtled through the window onto the bed one night, then turned round and spat. I rushed to the window, and just below it saw a fox, the size of an Alsatian.

I shouted, and it slunk away towards the wood. The ordinary, everyday fox, I am sure, does not catch cats. I once saw Lama sitting alongside a fox and it looked as if they were chatting, and not so long ago I saw a fox on one side of Monty's Leap, Ambrose on the other only a few feet away, and quite unperturbed. Only the rogue fox I worry about.

Thus I will sometimes wake up in the middle of the night, begin to worry, then force myself to leave the comfort of the bed and go to the spare room and see if Ambrose has returned. If the bed is empty, I will put on a dressing-gown and sleepily walk out into the night with a torch, and proceed to call: 'Ambrose! Ambrose!' Eventually he will appear, sometimes from the direction of Monty's Leap, the torch shining on a little shadow. Sometimes he will appear at my feet. He has listened to my shouts, my voice sounding more and more anxious, and all the while he has been in the *escallonia*, only a few yards away. Naturally, he always receives from me a rapturous welcome. I can go back to bed in peace.

A more serious menace than an imaginary rogue fox was about to appear. I had read about mink escaping from mink farms and creating havoc in their neighbourhoods, killing any animal or bird they set eyes upon. I had also heard rumours that mink had been seen in Lamorna Valley and

that prize peacocks had been killed by them, and chickens, and even a cat. I had read about these things, heard about them, but in the usual manner when one is not directly affected, they passed through my mind as if on a television screen. I observed, but emotionally it did not register.

Then one summer morning I went to Newlyn and to my friend Roger Veal from whom we buy our fish. After climbing up the rail-less steps into his store where the freshly collected fish from the harbour lie in boxes on the floor, I had to wait for him to finish a telephone conversation. I could not fail to listen to his end of this conversation and I was immediately startled by it.

'That's bad, that's terrible news!'

'Did you say a thousand of them?'

'At St Just... you mean someone left the gate open?'

'Yes, yes...'

'They'll be streaming down the river, spread everywhere.'

'Oh dear, terrible, terrible...'

I had come on my regular task of collecting coley for Ambrose and I was also collecting mackerel and lemon soles which Roger Veal would fillet for me. I was, however, distracted by the tone of his conversation. Some disaster seemed to have taken place. Roger Veal, a distinguished potter when not filleting fish, was not the kind of person who would inflate a crisis.

'You seem worried,' I said, as he put the telephone down, 'I couldn't help hearing your end of the conversation. What's the disaster?'

He took my question calmly, picking up a lemon sole, then a knife and beginning to fillet.

'Mink,' he said, 'they've burst out of a mink farm near St Just... a thousand are loose. They'll cause havoc.'

Instantly I was in a panic.

Roger Veal continued to fillet.

'Who told you all this?' I asked, and I was sounding

117

hysterical, thinking of the mink swarming across Monty's Leap, of our desperate efforts to keep Ambrose away from them, and thinking how the threat would never end, because they would breed and breed. The terrible thought enveloped me that the peaceful days of Ambrose at Minack were over.

'A reliable source,' said Roger Veal, 'she comes from Mousehole.'

The wads of coley, the mackerel wrapped up in newspaper, the lemon soles packed in thin paper, ready for the freezer. I was in such a hurry to leave that I said I would pay later.

What should I do? If a thousand mink were on their way I could not hold up my arms and stop them. What to do?

I hurried to Penzance police station and was soon in the waiting-room, pressing a button which announced my arrival. Through the windowframe of the waiting-room I saw a uniformed constable and a civilian. I waited, and waited, until, their particular business completed, the constable advanced measuredly to the glass door of the waiting-room, opened it and enquired politely what I wanted.

'It is about the mink,' I gushed, 'a thousand of them have escaped. You know all about it of course . . . they're going to cause chaos all over West Cornwall!'

'I've had no report about this,' said the constable, picking up a pen and preparing to take notes, 'if you will give me particulars. Where is this mink farm? How did you obtain this information?'

I explained and as he copied out my words, I was thinking of Ambrose. He would never be able to roam again, never be able to stroll up the lane on his own. A chill went through me as I thought of the strain that would be put on Jeannie and me as we tried to keep him indoors. Perhaps he would have to be put in a wire cage, as in a zoo. Or be kept in a greenhouse. The mink inevitably would make homes along the stream to Monty's Leap and around the now silted-up reservoir. Minack would be besieged.

'I will make enquiries,' said the constable solemnly, 'please come back in half an hour.'

I left the police station and walked out into the streets of Penzance, along Alverton to Market Place. Penzance is a gentle town, and though in summer the pavements are crowded, in the autumn after the holidaymakers have gone it becomes more like a huge village. No one is in a hurry. Shop assistants are friends. As you walk along the terrace of Market Jew Street, someone is sure to call out: 'How are you doing, my handsome?' or some other such greeting, and it is likely there will be many pauses for gossip. Only the buildings change in Penzance. Multiple stores have stretched their tentacles into the town, price-cutting out the old-established shops, taking their profits away from the town and up country across the Tamar. The old shops struggle to survive but one by one are dying out, often surrendering their quaintness to the brisk, functional appearance of a building society office.

It occurred to me that I could fill in the time by having my hair cut and so I went up the narrow street of Causewayhead, still a street of small shops, to the hairdressers where Bob Laing has cut my hair since I first came to Penzance. I admire the energy of hairdressers, standing all day, snipping, snipping, and coping with customers who chatter. I am not a chatterer but I am inclined, as I settle down in the chair, to ask Bob whether he has any special news of Penzance to give me, and he will answer 'nothing much'. He is very painstaking, and when I told him I hated electric clippers which shave the back of your head like a razor, he proceeded to buy a pair of hand clippers. At the end of each session, over the years, he has asked me the same question, a built-in question asked of any customer: 'Anything on?' He is referring to a hair lotion. As

119

if he has never asked me before I reply: 'No thanks.'

In London I once had a barber who was a very different person to Bob. He was an exiled Pole called Max and he was one of several barbers who worked in a well-known Bond Street hairdressing establishment. He was an excitable gentleman who developed a special yearning for my custom so that whenever I entered the establishment he rushed forward, whether he was busy or not, declaring that he, and not any of the other barbers, would look after me. His devotion was such that he began visiting Jeannie and me at our river home at Mortlake, bringing his wife, also Polish, a very quiet lady. Then one day, just before we left for Cornwall, an event took place as I sat in the chair, Max snipping at my hair, which was quite disturbing. He suddenly put down his scissors and picked up a barber's razor with its long blade; and then, like a clown performing a macabre joke, he slid it across my throat. He was laughing hysterically.

A couple of years after going to Cornwall I called again at this Bond Street establishment.

'Where's Max?' I asked, not seeing him around.

'He died,' came the answer, 'he was taken away to a mental hospital and he died there soon after.'

For some reason I had not been scared when he brandished his razor. I was, however, scared about the mink.

Bob was busy and could not give me an appointment, so I continued to wander until the half-hour was up for me to return to the police station.

'What news?' I asked anxiously, as soon as the constable appeared. He looked at me and there was a half-smile on his face, almost patronising, as if he was looking at someone who had made a fool of himself.

'I have made enquiries, Mr Tangye,' he said solemnly, 'and I have been in touch with the resident constable at St Just.'

He paused.

'There is, I understand, no mink farm at St Just,' he continued, 'and so there has been no escape of a thousand mink.'

I stared at him in astonishment . . . relieved, embarrassed.

'But I heard Roger Veal on the telephone and he said the story came from a reliable source.'

I was trying to justify myself.

'I have been in touch with Mr Veal and he says you must have been mistaken. As for his Mousehole source, we have been unable to make contact.'

I had been a fool, a panicky fool.

'Well,' I said in a matter-of-fact voice, hiding my shame, 'this means that my cat is safe and that was all that was worrying me.'

A couple of months later there was a sequel to this episode.

I was standing on the bridge, ruminating, when I saw something black move in the gap between the bridge and the Lama field. My immediate reaction was that I had seen a little black cat, and I dashed after it into the Lama field. It wasn't a black cat. It was a mink, the first I had ever seen. I stood still, and to my surprise instead of running away it came up to me, seemingly unafraid. It was a very pretty creature, and looking at its sleek black coat I thought with disgust of the mink farms where mink are imprisoned in cages, living artificially, all for the sake of vanity. It did not stay long. It loped quickly again to the gap, down the three steps to the bridge, through the *escallonia* and then past Annie's Folly and out of sight. I haven't seen a mink here since.

Nor, I must add, have I ever discovered the cause of that telephone conversation which led me to the police station with my account of the thousand escaping mink which never were.

Making a fool of yourself, however, doesn't do any harm

provided you don't allow your foolishness to escalate. At least you are showing your true feelings, in this case my feelings for Ambrose. There is a remark by Paul Renoir which long ago I made a note of. He spoke of: 'the eternal conflict between the intellect and feeling.' Then he added: 'I am on the side of feeling.'

He believed the intellect could be too calculating. The intellect, like a computer, stores knowledge and that although this knowledge is of great value, it can inhibit correct decision-making by stifling imagination. I once worked for a brilliant intellectual in MI5 who drove me to despair whenever a suspect came up for discussion. My friend would lucidly, convincingly, reel out intellectual reasons why the suspect could not be considered a suspect. My friend had no feeling, no intuition. A famous politician once said to me: 'A man can have brains, great wealth, great power... but without intuition he has nothing.'

I am, therefore, for the most part on the side of feeling. I prefer the person who has intuition and flair to the person who relies on the computer. The computer, the automatic intellect, will produce figures and facts that may satisfy a management who has asked for them, yet these facts and figures may be far from the truth. After all a computer has no imagination. It is operated by the finger-tip touch of a programmer who is working by rules. Thus a programmer who is comparing the sales in a shop between one week and the next will faithfully record the figures, but will fail to record the imponderables responsible for the results.

There are other aspects of the computer which breed a remoteness from reality, and we all suffer as a result in one way or another. In the world of entertainment, for instance, the computerised viewing figures rule over television screens, thus ensuring programmes of glossy predictability. Such programmes have their influence on other forms of entertainment. The obvious is more profitable than subtlety.

122

I am, however, faced with reality when I take out the Condor. I took it out one August evening and within a few minutes the engine spluttered to a stop. Over the years machines have often broken down at Minack and I have listened to numerous mechanics say in exasperation that the particular kind of breakdown was unique in their experience. Nor had any mechanic experienced the incident which took place shortly before the Condor broke down.

Jeannie one morning ran to tell me that no water was coming through the tap. I groaned, saying to myself that the well water which keeps us going through most of the year had dried up, and therefore we had to change over to the second supply that comes from the second well up the lane. The changeover meant a laborious switching of pipes and the installation of a pump which, for the rest of the year, I keep out of sight.

I decided, however, that first I had best check up on the normal supply tank. I found, as was to be expected, that the tank was empty. I then pressed a button at the side of the tank. Smoke curled up and I immediately switched off. Then I investigated the cause. A wire, it seemed, had fused, and I could see the wire, a thick wadge of it, and as far as my amateur electrician mind was concerned, that was that.

I thereupon went for help and the help which was available was my friend Mike Nichols who lives with his family in the cottage among the farm buildings at the top of the hill of our lane. He has his own business as a builder and repairer of all sorts, a craftsman in the old sense of the word. I hurried up the lane to see him before he set out on his day's work and within twenty minutes he was examining the small motor which drove my water pump.

'That is not a wire you see,' and he was pointing at what I had taken to be a wadge of wires, 'it is an adder!'

Adders are not unusual in our neighbourhood. From time to time I see one squirming across the grey chippings in front of the cottage then disappearing into a hole in the hedge. Then there was the occasion when Jeannie nearly sat on one. We have a small bench adjacent to a sheltered hedge in the Lama meadow and one lunchtime on a sunny day, a plate of sandwiches in her hand, Jeannie was about to sit down on it when I yelled: 'Look out!' A two-foot-long adder was resting there.

Some people have a phobia about adders, a terror of them. I myself used to kill them on sight, but over the years I have come to terms with them, Jeannie too. We have learnt that they will scurry away at the sight of a human and it is only when they are caught unawares that they are a danger. Thus, although we tolerate them, we are also on guard. We wear boots when we walk through undergrowth and, since the day I found one curled among the cucumbers in the greenhouse, I am wary as I go about my greenhouse business. The adder in the motor of my water pump had reached the motor through a gap beneath the wooden box that covered the pump. Had it been alive when I lifted the box, no doubt its reaction would have been to bite and I would not now be writing so tolerantly about adders.

I now had need of an electrician to examine the motor and assess the adder damage, and obviously I wanted this done as quickly as possible. Unfortunately, as many of us know, a speedy response from an electrician, a plumber or a builder is often difficult to achieve. A day and a time is promised, and you wait and you wait and you wait and the day passes without anyone appearing. Our particular electrician, however, did not usually allow us to suffer in this way, and we owe this, I believe, to Lord George Brown.

We were having dinner, George Brown, his wife Sophie, Jeannie and I, in the Lamorna Hotel one September evening before the 1964 election. George was having a brief holiday before the election, which was to lead to a Socialist triumph, a period of high office for George, then disillusionment. We were sitting at the table when the waitress came round with a bottle of red wine, but as she was filling George's glass someone knocked her arm holding the bottle – and the wine spurted over the table and on to George's jacket. The waitress was covered in confusion, but George immediately put her at her ease by making a joke of it. The waitress never forgot and she has shown her appreciation of that moment on many occasions since. Whenever we needed her husband, she saw that he came immediately. Her husband is our electrician.

On this occasion she was unable to help because she and her husband were away; and so for three days we kept calling them and there was no reply. However, I was to receive help from another source. From time to time, when I have been engaged in some form of home maintenance, I have had surprising help from visiting holidaymakers. For instance, one day I was patiently painting the white shutters of the cottage when a young man and his pretty wife appeared and, after a few words of welcome, I asked him what he did back home in Wigan. 'I'm a decorator,' he replied, then advancing towards me he added, 'give me the brush and I'll do the painting for you.' And he did.

Another day I was engaged in a plumbing job in the outside washroom and was having the greatest difficulty in unscrewing a pipe. I was about to admit failure when a charming couple from Dorking came down the lane, and again, after a few words of welcome, I asked the man what he did. 'I'm a plumber,' he said. So I explained my predicament. 'Leave it to me,' he answered cheerfully. An hour later, while I watched, my plumbing job was completed. Then a few months later my plumber friend returned. 'I noticed your wash basin had a crack,' he explained, 'so I've brought you a new one.' A gift.

Thus, whenever I am engaged on home maintenance, there lingers at the back of my mind the hope that someone suitable to the task upon which I am engaged may come down the winding lane. This was to happen as I waited for the electrician to return from his holiday. A couple from Bacup, who had visited us several times before, arrived and when in the course of conversation I told them about our adder in the motor and the absence of our electrician, the husband said: 'Didn't you know that I am an electrical engineer? I have my tools in the back of the car and it will only take me a short time to discover the damage the adder has done.' So it did. He removed the metal cover of the small motor and found that the adder had sabotaged it. It could not even be repaired. There was no alternative but to buy a new motor.

On warm summer evenings Jeannie and I have drinks up on the bridge and the sun shafts its light upon us, and often on Ambrose as well. In warm daytimes we are often in the grotto beside the bridge, and then Ambrose will lie in the grass of the old earth-built hedge, in the shade of the wild plum trees, like ourselves. It is when Ambrose is with us on these occasions that we experience the extraordinary relationship he has with birds. He never takes any notice of them. We crush a biscuit on a rock beside us and the regulars quickly arrive. Bossy Charlie chaffinch, Shelagh the lady chaffinch who is accompanied by offspring who expect her to feed them crumbs long after they are capable of pecking at them themselves. And there are the dunnocks, dim little brown birds like sparrows, and Toocan the blackbird with his bright yellow beak who pushes everyone away from the crumbs when he arrives. There is also Tabitha, a sleek mouse, who pops out of a hole when no birds are to be seen. Ambrose just blinks at them all. He is only impatient when a butterfly flutters too near to him, a grasshopper hops by, or a fly buzzes around him. Then a paw will make a useless gesture of attack.

We went up to the bridge one morning and toasted the arrival of the proof copy of Jeannie's *Bertioni's Hotel*.

Understandably, it was a precious moment for her to read in print the scenes which she had struggled so hard to create. A comparatively short book, describing twenty-four hours in the life of a London Hotel, a touching love story with an underlying theme of the value of standards.

At the same time as Jeannie was writing her book, our friend David Cornwell (John le Carré) was writing his novel of Middle East politics and intrigue called *The Little Drummer Girl*. We first knew him when he came to lunch a few years before and said he would like to have a holiday home in Cornwall. 'Well,' I said, 'do you hear that tractor? The farmer driving it has three cottages to sell all adjacent to each other.' David, between courses, walked across the fields to the farmer on his tractor, and bought the three cottages. One of them was where Jane, with the long fair hair, of *A Drake at the Door*, had lived when she worked for us. Curiously, David's wife is also called Jane, and also has long fair hair; and she too combines being very feminine with being very practical.

David will usually walk over to see us when making one of his visits, and he will bring bottles of wine, for he is a generous person, and the three of us have an intuitive understanding which results in periods of uninterrupted conversation. The kind of relaxing conversation which stimulates those taking part, no inhibitions, the true representation of friendship. Occasionally he arrives by car, and on one occasion as he left after having dinner with us, there was a ludicrous incident. He was about to set off, headlights blazing on the lane, when I suddenly saw it was the night of the frog mating season. Frogs crawled everywhere, an army of them down the lane from the cottage to Monty's Leap, and an odd sight resulted: David edged his way forward in the car while Jeannie and I, bent double, ushered the frogs to safety.

There were, therefore, these two contrasts on the Cornish

cliffs: David with his panoramic, painstakingly researched novel about the endemic strife in the world today, of the organised planning of deceit and murder; and further along the cliff Jeannie's tale of loyalty and love, and standards. It was ironic, as we were later to learn, that coincidentally both novels were to be published on the same day.

Meanwhile, however, we were sitting happily on the bridge toasting *Bertioni's Hotel*, discussing its prospects, making plans for its promotion, when we heard the sound of footsteps on the chippings, then voices.

'I'll see who it is,' said Jeannie.

I heard the murmur of her greeting, then she was back.

'It is Captain Ridley of the QE2,' she said; and behind her followed Captain Ridley, his wife and two pretty daughters.

NINE

Penny was alive when the QE2 first passed close to Minack. Its captain then was Captain Warwick and although I had never met him, he had written to say he would like to see Minack and that the QE2 would be passing by at 5 pm on a certain day, on the way from Cobh in Eire to Cherbourg. Could we put up some kind of identification? We decided to use a large orange tablecloth which we attached to a pole so it looked like a flag, and then stuck the pole in the ground of the field which ever since has been known as the QE2 field.

At 5 pm the QE2 slowly appeared a mile off shore. Jeannie and I were standing beside the orange tablecloth, and with us, on halters, were Penny and Fred. They were amazed. Fred has always shown great interest in boats. There he will be munching grass in one of the meadows

overlooking the sea when he will stop munching, be suddenly alert, and all because some boat is passing by that he does not recognise. Obviously he could not be expected to recognise the QE2. Hence when she suddenly came into view, sailing down the coast from Lands End, so graceful yet so massive, Fred could not restrain himself from hooting in excitement. Simultaneously the sirens of the QE2 roared a greeting to us. So there we were beside our orange tablecloth witnessing the only known occasion when a QE2 greeting was answered by a donkey's hoot.

It was a different situation, however, when the QE2 passed by a few years later. We had not been warned. I was standing on the bridge one early November afternoon when I suddenly saw the outline of this great liner, close inshore, sailing westwards from the direction of Penzance. I raced to the cottage.

'The QE2!' I shouted to Jeannie who was in the cottage, kneading the dough of the weekly bread, 'the QE2 is coming!'

What we did not know at the time was that the QE was on a short mystery cruise between her normal famous sailings. Nor did we know that the current captain was Captain Ridley who had been First Officer when the QE2 received hoots from Penny and Fred, on that first occasion she passed by Minack.

'Get the donkeys!' was the cry from Jeannie, her hands sticky with dough. 'I'll be with you in a second!'

I often wonder how I would react if the cottage caught on fire. A dramatic urgency forcing a quick decision. Which of the paintings would I first try to save? Surely Kanelba's portrait of Jeannie would be the first because it had been with us for all our married life, and before. But I would also have to seize Jeannie's own painting of Ambrose on his rock; and there were the exquisite John Miller pictures which we had collected over the years; and John Armstrong's; and that of the River Thames from a fourth floor suite of the Savoy Hotel which Jeannie commissioned

Julian Phipps to do for a Savoy Christmas card. There were others of Jeannie's own paintings: the cornfield spreading before the farmhouse at the top of the lane; Lama when we first saw her, hiding in the meadow where we grew marigolds; and Monty, painted on the last day of his life. All these pictures would have to be saved if I was suddenly faced with a fire emergency.

And what of the furniture, and the books, and the various china ornaments, and items like the first copy of Karsh's famous photograph of Churchill given to Jeannie by Karsh himself before he even gave one to Churchill? That would have to be saved, so too another photograph of Churchill signed by himself, and also the compass which A. P. Herbert had at Gallipoli and which he kept on his famous Thames boat *The Water Gypsy*; and also the pottery cat which Howard Spring bought in Manchester to celebrate his first success, *Shabby Tiger*. All such items I would have to remember to save.

The sofa I would have to forget, the sofa which has been part of my life since I was a child. So too the dresser which my mother bought for us when first we came to the cottage. So too the tallboy whose drawers bulge with our photographs over the years, but I would have to try to save the photographs. The wine bin I could save, easy to carry. But what about my kidney-shaped Regency desk? Would I be able to get it through the door in time? And the books. Each time a Minack Chronicle has been published my publishers have generously given me a leather-bound copy done by the famous binder Sagorski. These must be saved. But as for the rest of the books, I visioned myself hurling them out of the window, seizing them at random from the shelves.

'The QE2 is coming!'

I rushed out to get the donkeys, then realised they were not in the neighbourhood, neither in the stable meadow nor in the donkey field. They were in the clover field on Oliver land . . .

'Jeannie,' I cried out, 'you get the donkeys. They're in the clover field, quick. I'll find the cameras and the orange flag and the pole, then I'll come and help you.'

Jeannie rushed past me, sticky doughy hands forgotten.

I picked up Jeannie's camera, checked the lever and it jammed. I picked up my own camera: there was no film in it. I had a spare one somewhere, couldn't find it.

Then I went outside.

The QE2 was slowly advancing towards us, approaching Carn Barges, that collection of granite rocks from where we first saw Minack.

'Derek!' came Jeannie's voice from a distance.

Then thundering down the lane came the donkeys.

And Jeannie chasing them, a moment later.

'Catch them,' she said, 'catch them!'

But Merlin had diverted his route and run through the gap to the Orlyt and the orchard. Fred had chosen another direction. He had sped past me joyously, the usual kind of Fred who has broken loose from normal routine, and then dashed into the donkey field, kicking up his legs.

Jeannie and I were desperate.

Fred in the donkey field.

Merlin in the orchard.

The QE2 sailing inexorably towards us.

'I've got him!'

Jeannie's cry was exultant.

So it was up to me . . . to catch Fred.

'Come Fred,' I said, softly, standing by the gateway of the donkey field, 'come Fred, dear Fred . . . don't you want to hoot at the QE2 again?'

He succumbed.

Thus Jeannie and I raced the donkeys to the QE2 field.

The QE was edging past Carn Barges.

'What about the orange flag? The whole point is to have it!'

I had left it by the gate and I ran back and fetched it.

The QE was now opposite us, in the exact position when on the last occasion Fred and Penny hooted. No hoots this time. Fred seemed to have been startled into silence by the rush of events. As for Merlin, he had escaped from his halter and, after rushing round the field in joyous freedom, he turned his back on the QE2. As far as he was concerned, she could be ignored.

Perhaps, however, there was a reason for such behaviour. Had he shown interest, had he infected Fred with the same excitement that Penny had done, Fred might have hooted, and if that was the case he would have been expected to hoot as well.

But he couldn't hoot.

Never in his life has he been able to hoot.

Captain Ridley, having seen Minack from the sea, was wanting to see the sea from Minack. He wanted to meet the donkeys and have a look at our orange flag, and so I found the orange flag (or tablecloth) and we took it to the QE2 field and Captain Ridley's two pretty daughters took photographs. Everyone co-operating except Merlin.

I reflect, sometimes, on the way that people, particularly business people, can travel today compared with the industrial pioneers of a hundred years ago. Today in luxury, and with great speed, while a hundred years ago they sailed their long journeys in ships much smaller than present-day cross-Channel boats.

My grandfather was one such pioneer. He died long before I was born, and as I grew up I was led to believe that he was a very difficult person. My mother, I regret, was mainly responsible for this impression. My mother was the epitome of a perfect mother, always entering into our enthusiasms, always willing to make any personal sacrifice if, by so doing, she made me or my brothers happy. But she never liked my grandfather. And the cause was a simple one. When she became engaged to my father, she set out to win my grandfather by exercising her charm on him. My grandfather was not impressed. He, like many a father, questioned the suitability of this new entry into the family, and he distrusted the way my mother behaved towards him. So unfair on my mother – she only wanted to be made welcome by him.

Perhaps there were other reasons why I was not made aware of the greatness of my grandfather, for I realise now that he was, in that late-Victorian era, one of the great pioneers. Perhaps such reasons were created by myself. I do not remember having any curiosity about my grandfather. He was a distant person in my youthful mind, a 'funny little man with a white beard' as my mother described him, and I showed not the slightest interest in the story of his rise from being the son of a shopkeeper and smallholder in the Cornish village of Illogan to being, in the company of his three brothers, the creator of Cornwall Works in Birmingham where at the turn of the century two thousand men were employed. Perhaps there was one particular reason for my lack of interest: by the time I had reached the age when I could be expected to be aware of him, the Tangye engineering fortunes had collapsed. As so often happens in a family firm, the third generation had failed and so there was no spur to make me admire him.

My attitude, however, was to change. Apart from his achievement in helping to create a section of the industrial revolution, apart from his pioneer journeys abroad (eight times to Australia and New Zealand) during which he made Tangyes a household name all over the world, he was a very enlightened reformer. He introduced the nine-hour day for his work people, was the first industrialist to have a works' canteen and to have free medical facilities for all his employees. He was a generous benefactor and he and his brother George substantially helped towards the cost of the Birmingham Art Gallery. He was a radical and a fervent admirer of Gladstone who pressed him to enter politics – and indeed there were twenty occasions when he was offered safe seats. But a political career did not interest him, he believing his gifts were of more use in the real world. He refused many honours and only reluctantly in the end accepted a knighthood. He was also an admirer of Cromwell and wrote a book about him called *Two Protectors*. His collection of Cromwellian relics was the finest in the country.

He was, therefore, a very distinguished person and had many friends. But, like my mother, I do not think I would have warmed to him. He was too straightlaced, too much of a Puritan, a man to admire but not to be at ease with. Recently I received a parcel which shows a curious side to his character.

Like all my family, he was a dog man. He had a succession of dogs and to each one he was devoted, and each one was treated as a special friend. When they died they were buried in a corner of our Cornish home near Newquay with suitable inscriptions on wooden crosses. But in the later period of his life he had a very special favourite which he called Little Gyp and about whom he published an essay. Little Gyp was very small, her body being only about twelve inches in length, and she apparently was of the Italian greyhound species. He first saw this dog under unusual circumstances. He was leaving Adelaide after one of his visits to Australia and a farewell party took place on board. In the mêlée of the occasion this little dog was accidentally left on board by one of the farewell partygoers.

My grandfather who, I am quite sure, had taken no part in any farewell party, observed this little dog a day or two later walking about the deck in the company of an elderly lady fellow-passenger. He thought it was the most beautiful little dog he had ever seen and he remembered how, before his journey to Australia, he had promised his daughter that one day he would give her a dog. This was the dog, he said to himself, and as someone who had struggled his way to eminence, who had won victories by ruthless determination, he was not going to be thwarted.

He was to have luck on his side. The lady concerned, though adopting the little dog, giving her a home in her cabin, feeding her and behaving during the course of the voyage as if she now owned her, made one mistake. The captain of the vessel (called *Orient*) demanded five guineas for the fare to England and the elderly lady refused to pay it. My grandfather thereupon asked the captain what would happen to the little dog if the fare was not paid and the captain, in his reply, inferred that she would be destroyed. My grandfather now asked that the lady should be requested once more to pay the fare and said if she did not agree to do so he would pay it – and then he would consider that the dog belonged to him. The lady was asked. She refused again and the captain agreed that the dog was now my grandfather's.

I would have thought that my grandfather, being such a high-minded person, would have told the lady what he had done. He did not do so, but allowed her to continue as if she owned the dog until the end of the voyage. He then arranged for the dog to be kidnapped the night before the *Orient* was due in Plymouth and then taken away to London. The elderly lady, I gather, was distraught. As far as she knew the dog might have leapt overboard.

However, my grandfather was going to cosset this dog he called Little Gyp, and there is no doubt that for twelve years she had the kind of life that unluckier dogs dream about. But had I been my grandfather, the lady on the *Orient* would have remained on my conscience. She was never on his. In his essay he describes a visitor who came to his Cornish home when Little Gyp trotted into the room. 'What a beautiful little dog!' the visitor said, 'it is just like one a lady friend of mine lost on board ship as she was returning from Australia!' What was in the parcel which prompted me to tell this story?

The grandfather of the sender had been a spare-time gardener for my grandfather, and the latter, after Little Gyp died, gave him Little Gyp's small green and white celluloid collar with a bell . . . possibly because, as a gardener, he may have dug the grave of Little Gyp. It was this collar with a bell which was in the parcel. On receiving it, I read again a passage in the essay which may suggest that my grandfather was not as straightlaced as I have said. He wrote, sentimentally, as follows:

Mr Jesse, whom I have quoted before, says that dogs know when they are going to die, and when dying take a last farewell, affection showing supremely at the last moment of existence. So it was with my faithful little friend. She had been lying in her blanket before the fire, breathing heavily while I was writing at my desk by the window, when she presently got up and came towards me with feeble, tottering steps, and gave me such a loving and pathetic look. I felt that the end had come, and, lying down by her side, she fell on my arm, and in a few seconds had breathed her last.

I now believe that the elderly lady of the *Orient* would have approved of the future that lay ahead for the little dog which was her companion during that voyage from Australia, had she known. For my part I will always be grateful to the sender of Little Gyp's collar.

I have received other echoes of my grandfather. The son

of a one-time servant sent me a bellows which was once kept beside the fireplace in the drawing-room of Coombe Bank, near Kingston-on-Thames where my grandfather also had a home. I have also had a copy or two of his privately printed autobiography called *One and All* and the other day I received a copy from Canada of his *Tales of a Grandfather*. I have others of his privately printed books and the contents have a gentle humour, laced with comments which bore witness to his Cromwellian beliefs. A good man, for certain, but not cosy.

The two donkeys had other excitements in the QE2 field besides observing activities on the sea. They acted, for instance, as watch-donkeys: if we happened to see them standing, ears pointed, staring at some aspect of our land, they immediately alerted us that something odd was going on. One warm summer evening they were particularly helpful in this respect although, to be accurate, it wasn't pointed ears which alerted us but Fred's hoot.

About six o'clock three young men arrived at the door with a large plastic bottle, asking for water. They had walked up from the coastal path and as I filled the bottle I asked them where they were walking to. They were foreign and seemed to have difficulty in understanding my question. After I had repeated it, one of them replied that they were not going any further but were going to camp in a field beside the coastal path. I was immediately on guard. Casual campers are banned by owners of land beside the coastal path unless special permission is given, and the reason is easy to understand. Apart from the litter problem, damage to crops, and sanitation, there are new factors to be considered in the climate of today's society. People living in lonely places, therefore, do not welcome strangers camping in their neighbourhood.

So I explained my attitude to the three young men,

adding that there was an authorised campsite three miles further on where they would be assured of a welcome. They countered my remarks by saying they had three girls with them whose feet were so sore after walking many miles that they could not walk any further. I remained adamant that they could not camp in the neighbourhood. I also had a sixth sense that they were not telling the truth. They seemed to accept my point of view and off they went with their bottle of Minack well water.

Jeannie and I were having cold roast beef with lettuce and potato salad that evening, and so there was no cooking to be done. It was very warm and Jeannie was still in her shorts.

'Let's peel the Cape gooseberries,' I said suddenly, 'we can go up on the bridge and we'll do the work with the help of a bottle of wine.'

I had picked the Cape gooseberries two days before and they had been a splendid crop. I have two rows of plants, each two feet apart in the rows, in one of the greenhouses. I had grown them from seed four years before and had left them *in situ* ever since, cutting them down to ground level after each fruiting season, and of course keeping the soil between the plants free of weeds. By March they begin to grow again, by June they are four feet tall and spreading their stems out like an umbrella with untidy yellow flowers on them. By July the flowers are enclosed in a green, paper-like cocoon which soon turns a pale yellow while the fruit within ripens into the size of a conventional gooseberry.

Jeannie has always had a particular weakness for them. Her weakness began when she was at the Savoy where she would frequently be entertaining distinguished people for lunch or dinner, and when a waiter at the end of such a meal placed a plate of *friandises* on the table, Jeannie always asked for Cape gooseberries to be among them. Each fruit had been dipped in icing sugar with white of egg to make it bind, and the paper-like cocoon, peeled back from the fruit, was twisted into a stem which you held. We had other uses, however, now that we grew them in quantity. They were, for instance, delicious when stewed; and so, after harvesting the crop, after removing the paper-like cocoon, Jeannie packed them in polythene bags and put them in the freezer.

It was a soothing, mindless task removing the cocoons. On this hot summer evening we sat there in the grotto beside the bridge, a heap of Cape gooseberries on the glass top of the garden table, leisurely putting the fruit in one basket, the

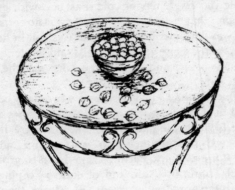

discarded cocoons in another. Ambrose was on a seat beside us, taking no notice of Shelagh the chaffinch as she flighted in the wild plum tree branches that covered the grotto like a canopy. We talked inconsequently, sometimes silent, listening to the sad late summer song of a robin, or the cry of a curlew, or the bellow-sounding beat of a gull's wings, or the background murmur of the sea. Gentle sounds. Then suddenly from the direction of the QE2 field came a very excitable hoot.

We continued with our task. We were at peace. We did not want to be disturbed.

A minute later there were more hoots, urgent hoots, desperate hoots.

'Poor Fred,' said Jeannie, 'he sounds terribly upset.'

The stress in his hoot reminded me of that night after Penny had died. Something really was upsetting him.

'I'll go and investigate,' I said, 'I won't be a minute.'

I walked down past the barn, through the gate, then the gap into the QE2 field and saw at the far end the backsides of Fred and Merlin. I hurried towards them and as I did so Fred's hoot had become hysterical. Merlin, hootless Merlin, was in such a state of excitement that he was pawing at the ground, then racing away for a few yards, then racing back. And no wonder.

A large tent had been erected in the centre of the meadow below the QE2 field, the meadow where we grow daffodils called Sulphur. In other parts of the meadow were smaller tents. And I suddenly realised that the three young men who had called at the cottage for water, who had told me that they had three girls with sore feet who could not walk any further, were in fact members of a party of thirty to forty who had decided that the Sulphur meadow was a suitable place to camp for the night. It was understandable why Fred and Merlin were furious.

I stood there between them, Fred hooting, me silent. I was flummoxed.

'Hey,' I at last called out, 'you can't camp there!'

A feeble order.

No one took any notice.

'I said you can't camp there!'

I have often wondered how a policeman feels when he faces a crowd with only his moral authority, and a baton.

Unruliness, vandalism and aggression may be endemic in today's society, but it is silly to pretend that they are unique for this age. There was a cabin in the grounds of our home near Newquay which was built snugly into the cliff above the entrance to Porth Bay. It had thick glass windows and we would sit in the cabin while a storm raged outside, watching the killer waves coming nearer and nearer until they exploded on the rocks beneath, sending their spray crashing against the glass windows. But it wasn't only the spray of killer waves which crashed against the windows. Twice, during my schooldays, vandals crashed stones against those windows, breaking them.

'You're on my daffodil ground,' I shouted, 'you're trespassing, you're causing damage!'

Two men began playing guitars. Another made a Harvey Smith sign. A young woman in a mother earth costume held up a beer can as if she was pretending to drink my health. Then I smelt a strange scent wafting up from the meadow, not the sea scent to which I was accustomed. I now had a bright idea. I hurried back to Jeannie, leaving Fred to carry on his hooting, and told her what was happening. 'Your camera,' I said, 'that will deal with the situation. You join the donkeys and take the pictures. I'll go down the path and face up to them.'

My arrival at the Sulphur meadow coincided with Jeannie's arrival on the QE2 field, and as I stood there one of the young men who had come to the cottage walked up to me. I kept calm.

'You lied,' I said cheerfully.

'I'm sorry.'

'You must leave.'

Out of the corner of my eye I saw Jeannie pointing her camera at me, pointing the camera at the tents all round the meadow.

'You see my wife up there with the donkeys? She's taking photographs of you all.'

The young man returned to his comrades, the guitars stopped playing and there was a sudden flurry of activity, and instead of tents being erected, tents were being dismantled. Soon with packs on their backs, they began tramping away towards the official campsite an hour away.

142

But before they left the young man came up to me again.
'We are friends, yes?' he asked.
And we shook hands.

TEN

There was no autumn this year at Minack. Late summer turned into winter overnight when a westerly raged for forty-eight hours early in October.

I had gone for a walk along the coastal path across our land to Carn Barges in the late afternoon, and when I reached Carn Barges I sat on the corner of the plinth upon which the Carn stands, where Monty once sat, the edge of which was once smashed by overkeen members of a mining college who were seeking specimens of Cornish rocks.

I sat there, and the late afternoon was benign. A gentle sea, a clear sky except for a roll of billowy clouds far away in the direction of the Scillies. A skin diver's speedboat slid across the water like an insect. The dying sun caught the cabin window of a boat so that it blazed like a searchlight. A raven, high to my right, nagged a buzzard. I heard the distant croak of a pheasant and guessed it was on one of the paths I had cut with the Condor. Then to the east of Lamorna Cove I saw two of the fishing trawlers of Newlyn, grey, white foam around their bows, thrusting their way out of Mounts Bay towards distant fishing grounds. Then just beside me, spreadeagled in the sun on a lichen-covered rock, the brilliant red, white and black colours of a Red Admiral butterfly. It was not one that would migrate. Too late for that. It would hibernate in some corner of these Cornish cliffs or in a farm building.

The migration of frail butterflies is even more wondrous than the migration of tiny warblers. Details about the distance they travel are scarce because, obviously, butterflies cannot be marked in the way birds can be ringed. It is known, however, that the Painted Lady butterfly that arrives on the southern coast of England in late May comes from Algeria and that many will travel there in the autumn. There are other travellers like the Clouded Yellow, the Camberwell Beauty, the Large White and, of course, the Red Admiral. But the week before that late afternoon I was sitting on Carn Barges, I saw one of the rarest travellers of all.

When I was young I used to collect butterflies, encouraged to do so by one of my schoolmasters. I used to race around the countryside with my butterfly net, swooping joyfully on any butterfly I could see, then proceed to carry out the macabre routine of asphyxiating it in a special jar, then pinning it proudly on a board. I aimed to be a great butterfly collector, perhaps presenting my collection one day to a museum so that, in stuffy rooms, people could stare at these beautiful creatures that were caught in the high noon of a summer's day. Of course I now look back upon my behaviour with horror, yet, to be fair to myself, I have to remember that what I did was in innocence. Actions that lead to regret are often performed in innocence.

I caught sight of my rarest of butterfly travellers one late September morning when I came out of my office, which I call my confusion room after a session of office work, and saw, high up in the *escallonia* bush on the other side of the lane, a patch of colour the size of a wren. I was so aware that I was looking at something very unusual that I quickly turned back and picked up a pair of fieldglasses. Then, focussing on this patch of colour, I saw it was a huge butterfly.

I have a number of reference books dealing with the identity of birds, of wild flowers, of mammals, of trees, of the mushroom family, of wild plants, of butterflies... but I have found that whenever the emergency has arisen that I have wanted to identify the subject I am interested in, I am unable to do so. The colour of the feathers seems to be different, the shape of the leaf, the design of the butterfly wings. Here I am, surrounded by books whose authors set out to make identification easy to understand, and I am nonplussed.

It did not, however, take me long to identify the butterfly that was resting on the leaf of the *escallonia* bush, because its size was unique in the butterfly world. It was a Monarch – and it had no right to be in this country. Its home was America and it normally spent the summer in the states of New Hampshire and New York, then, with the coming of winter, it flew 1500 miles south to the warmth of Louisiana and the Gulf States of America. An extraordinary voyage in itself. But how did this Monarch come to be resting on the leaf of the *escallonia* at Minack?

The Monarch is also a resident of the Canary Islands so it might be reasonable to assume that it came from there. There is, however, certain proof that it had not done so. Other sightings of Monarchs in the south-west were

reported beside my personal Monarch, and this caused the butterfly experts to look for the reason for this unusual invasion. In 1933 there had been 40 sightings, in 1968 there were 65. On this occasion there were nearly 100, although many may have been duplicate sightings.

The experts studied the weather conditions and they found that at the time that the migration of the Monarchs from the states of New York and New Hampshire to the south began, there were very strong westerly and south-westerly winds blowing in the area around a very deep depression. This depression swept across the Atlantic and was over Britain within four days. The experts came to the conclusion that the Monarchs came with the depression. My Monarch on the *escallonia* leaf, therefore, had flown the Atlantic in four days. The Monarch rested on the leaf for ten minutes, then fluttered its way across the top of the Orlyt to the cherry tree which grows higher and higher without producing any cherries. For a while I lost sight of it, and by this time I had called Jeannie, and so we were both looking for it. Jeannie now saw it for the first time and she was amazed by its size. She caught sight of it as it flew away from the cherry tree towards Monty's Leap and Oliver land.

I am not usually a meticulous person, but on this occasion I made a note of the time of the Monarch's arrival, the length of time in our sight and the direction in which it flew when it left us. I then reported these details to the County Museum at Truro and was rewarded by the intense interest of the curator. As a result I was to see my name, in due course, mentioned in the important scientific organ, the *Entomologist's Record*. The report of the sightings of the Monarch included this sentence:

Lamorna, seen for ½ hour about noon Sept. 28. mostly on escallonia. Photographed; flew westwards (D. Tangye per RDP, Curator Truro Museum)

The operative word is 'photographed'.

No question of chasing a rare, beautiful butterfly with a net. I had caught its beauty forever with a camera.

There I was sitting on the corner of the plinth of Carn Barges on this benign late afternoon when a gust of wind suddenly, momentarily, touched me and then went on towards Lamorna, leaving the air around me still again. I was instinctively aware that it was a warning. A change in the weather was on the way. The gale which was to last for forty-eight hours was about to begin.

When a gale is over I go out to look what damage has been done, expecting it. The greenhouses, of course, are always vulnerable. There is one greenhouse, the oldest one, which is a particular problem. Over the years parts of the frames have rotted and the glass panels have slipped or broken. I have patched the gaps up with polythene sheets, but then a gale comes and loosens the sheets so that they wave in the gale like flags. I do not know what to do about this greenhouse. Sometimes we say we will dismantle it, but there are so many other things to do other than dismantling a greenhouse; and so it continues to stand there, battered, yet surviving.

It survived again this gale. The casualty on this occasion was the small greenhouse where we bunch daffodils. Two panels of the roof had been smashed and the glass scattered over the benches, and two panels on the side had also been smashed, and here the glass had scattered on the grass where Ambrose often hunted. Our first task, after the gale was over, was laboriously to pick up the glass fragments both outside and inside the greenhouse.

Around this greenhouse and in the wood are the elms, some already bare of leaves due to the Dutch elm disease, but some still burgeoning green leaves... until the gale came. There were no green leaves after the gale, and the salt that came with it. The leaves turned black and became brittle like wafer-thin potato crisps. There were other casualties, and when Jeannie and I walked around Oliver land, green with late summer forty-eight hours before, the scene was sad. The change had been too sudden. It was as if one had been suddenly bereaved. The long summer soothingly making one pretend that there was never any end to time, and now the awakening.

There were compensations. The days went by and, without being self-conscious, without even knowing within myself that I had changed in my attitude, I began to be aware of another form of beauty in the land around us after the gale had raged.

Swallows still appeared over our land, late starters on their journey to South Africa. Bracken became red-brown reminding me of Monty and the description I gave of him when I first saw him: the colour of autumn bracken. True, the summer house of the donkeys where they liked to shelter on hot summer days now looked as if the roof had been blown off, the roof having consisted of the dense foliage of the elderberry tree. But in its place, around the elderberry tree, I was able to look at the beginning of next year's foxgloves, broad green leaf clumps, immune to a gale. It had turned warm after the storm. Hover flies appeared again and deceived butterflies, and cobwebs stretched across the narrow paths, and Jeannie when we walked along them, demanded that I should go first. Daddy-long-legs were too numerous and they would come indoors, bashing themselves against a tablelamp, and Jeannie would tell me to capture the offender, capture it gently, then open the door and let it fly away – let it turn into a leather jacket which will proceed to nibble at the roots of some plant I have grown. There were still blackberries to be picked. The donkeys enjoyed coming with us to pick them, and there would sometimes be arguments because an outstretched donkey neck reached a clump first. There were also the sloes. It had been a bad year for sloes because frost in May had cut the blackthorn flowers, and so we were glad to be able to pick enough of the survivors to enable us to have our annual sloe gin vintage. Last year's vintage had been a disaster. The fermenting jar had been carefully placed in my confusion room. One day, looking for something in the confusion, I had kicked it and the jar broke. Jeannie, who was responsible for the jar, who had picked the sloes, who had also pricked them, who had poured in the sugar and the two bottles of gin which was to make five bottles of liqueur, was not pleased.

Our flowerbeds are sheltered from the westerlies by the cottage, and so after the gale a visitor would say in a surprised tone: 'Still colour in the garden.' Our garden, however, does not please those gardeners who admire neatness. Our garden is disorganised, deliberately so because it means the cottage looks as if it is naturally growing out of moorland and the rocks of moorland. This casualness is not the result of lack of effort because Jeannie works hard on the garden. But neither of us, for instance, believes that weeds should be treated like vermin, or that grass growing on a path is evil.

Weeds seem to me to provoke a form of horticultural class warfare. Weeds are belowstairs, flowers are above-stairs. I have often wondered how it was decided what should be flowers, and what should be weeds; and why it should be that, unlike the Man-made social scene, weeds have never been able to edge their way upwards in the garden social scene. Why should the yellow of a dandelion be considered belowstairs? Or a daisy which has chosen to appear on a lawn? Or what is wrong with the purple flower of a knapweed unless one has long been brainwashed into believing that one has committed a social error by not pulling it up?

I have many favourite weeds once I rid myself of my guilt

that they should not be there. I like the little blue flowers of speedwell, and although I may claw at the roots of a buttercup before it flowers, I revel in the sight of it when it does so in patches of the rose garden. I am loath to remove foxgloves, although they may take up a patch of ground where I wish to plant wallflowers. I always leave pink campion and its spreading pink flowers, wherever the clump may be; and I am even inclined to leave the brilliant white flower of the greedy bindweed as it twines its way up any object it can find.

I mislead, however, if I have given the impression that weeds predominate in our garden. In spring it is a blaze of daffodils and early-flowering wallflowers and polyanthus, and forget-me-nots, and ascania violets, and aubretia. There follow arcotis and alyssum, and tobacco plants, and tulips, and mignonette and marigolds.

Our garden is beautiful to look upon in early summer but trouble begins in July. It begins when the alstroemeria has finished flowering and there has been a dry spell. Alstroemeria, along with montbretia, is a curse in a small garden. Both spread out of control just as oxalis spreads. Yet each of them have their moments of glory. Alstroemeria, below the pale-blue waterbutt, is a mass of orange and yellow flowers in July. Montbretia during the same period in various corners displays its spindly red blooms, while the oxalis is a flood of pink on the earthy ledge above the white seat, except on dull days when the petals refuse to open. Yet, except for the oxalis which will continue to bloom, the other two must be pulled up when their flowering stops, especially the alstroemeria which covers its area with a mass of dull green leaves. How does one fill the vacant space is our perennial question? And how does one fill the space left by the wallflowers when they have finished flowering?

I envy those gardeners who seem to cope with such

problems so easily. They succeed in organising in succession a spring garden, a summer garden and an autumn garden, without any of the plants overlapping the others. We have the additional problem of shallow soil which quickly dries out in any dry spell. So when July comes there is always the likelihood of parched plants and vacant spaces. At this stage we are ashamed of our garden and all we can murmur is: 'You should have seen it in spring.'

But this year I had a brainwave. I am sure lots of people have had the same brainwave and I only wish I had had it before in previous summers. Jeannie and I proceeded to become instant gardeners. We went off to see William Hocking, who was once the young assistant of Percy Potter when Percy Potter was the head gardener of the Sutton Seed Trial Gardens at Gulval just outside Penzance. Suttons gave up these trial grounds and by that time Percy Potter had died, and so William Hocking, Scillonian born, set up his own nursery. He had been well trained. Percy Potter had been one of those gardeners who *felt* about growing, even considered this sense of feeling more important than knowledge. Over the years Jeannie and I used to visit him, and listen.

It is a fascinating fact about the true and experienced gardener that he is never dogmatic. Their advice is gentle, easily accepted, though it may not be implemented. Percy Potter was one of those gardeners. How often I have recalled one piece of advice he gave us, although it didn't sound like advice in the strict meaning of the word. We were talking about flowers that grow in the summer, any flowers, and Percy said, pipe in his mouth: 'Give them a hair cut, they'll come on again.'

We returned from William Hocking with trays of plants in small ochre-coloured pots, among them busy lizzie, dwarf fuchsias, begonias and pansies. We placed them in strategic points where the soil was barren, and in the space

152

left by the torn-up, tired-looking leaves of the alstroemeria; and then we dug the pots into the ground, hiding them well with soil up to the rim. Within an hour we had a garden we could be proud of for the rest of the summer, and all we had to do during a dry spell was to water the pots. True, I felt guilty sometimes by this deception, but then one can feel guilty about any trivial matter if one is in the mood.

The gale had flattened areas of bracken so that they resembled brown lakes; and this worried me because the time was near when I should have to start cutting down the bracken and the undergrowth on the daffodil meadows and it is far harder work when the bracken is flattened. I sweep the motorised Brush Cutter to and fro in the small meadows and use the Condor mowing machine in the fields. I have satisfaction when I have done it because I can observe my achievement: a mess of a meadow one moment, a clean one the next. Any worker is happier when he can see what he has achieved – and I am always reminded of this simplistic view when I see Walter Grose, the Pied Piper of cats.

He has been a farmer all his life and for many years he has been a partner of my friend Jack Cockram, and farming the land all around Minack. Walter has watched the revolution in farming, from horsedrawn ploughs and natural feeding of soil and cattle to giant tractors, chemical fertilisers and scientific feeding. He still, however, prefers the pleasure of a sickle with which to cut back a hedge, or the use of a fork to spread manure. In all weathers you may see him out in the fields, or coming back at the end of the day, two muddy dogs at his heels, Trigger the spaniel and Whisky the one-eyed black and white collie. Jeannie met him up the lane the other day in the late afternoon and instead of wearing his usual hat he was bareheaded, holding his hat like a plate. It was full of mushrooms.

'Have them,' he said, offering the hat to Jeannie, and

when she refused them because he had picked them for himself, he added: 'Plenty more on the far side of that field above you. Don't want to see them wasted. Go and take what you want.'

He is a bachelor and we tease him about this.

'Nobody wants me,' is his reply.

'But Walter you're so good-looking and easy to get on with!'

And so the banter goes on.

On Mondays I take up the dustbins to the top of the lane and leave them there to be collected the following morning. Sometimes, if I go at teatime, I see Walter sitting in his yellow van feeding his cats. On one such Monday I joined him and found him in a serious mood.

'Went to a funeral last week,' he said, 'made me think. All the work I've done here over the years, all be forgotten when I go.'

'You've years ahead of you, Walter.'

'I was looking at those gravestones, hard working people they were once, fifty, a hundred years ago. All forgotten.'

'Cheer up,' I said, as a tabby rubbed against my leg, 'they're probably having a better time than they had on earth.'

'Do you believe in heaven and hell?'

'Not exactly ... I've got my own theory as to what happens when we die.'

'What's that?'

I told him, jokingly, that I likened heaven and hell to two mammoth industrial organisations.

'Look around you,' I said, 'and think of the millions and millions of things that have to be created on this planet, from the minutest insect to the clouds in the sky. Think of the multitude of animals and birds and all their different forms and colours, think of the population, think of the nasty things like diseases.' One of the cats had jumped on to

154

the bonnet of the yellow van and was elegantly washing itself.

'So it's my theory,' I went on, 'that when we die we become members of these mammoth organisations and are given the tasks to perform for which we are best suited.'

'In heaven or hell?'

'Well,' I said, 'those who go to heaven are employed in making all the nice things, those who go to hell make all the nasty things.'

'What do you think they'll make me do?'

'Easy to answer,' I replied, 'you and Jeannie will be allocated to the department that designs the coats of cats.'

Walter looked at me, and smiled.

'Just a joke, Walter,' I said.

There used to be three farms spreading out from the ancient buildings beside one of which Walter sat in his van. No one I know can tell me the age of these buildings, but it is fair to believe that the site on which they stand has been in use for farming for a thousand years or more. A tiny chapel was once discovered close by, but at the time of the discovery there was not the interest that exists today in relics of the past and it was destroyed.

Such ancient buildings do not exude the right image for modern farming; and I suppose if, to all our dismay, a technocrat farmer took over, he would drive a bulldozer through the buildings and start again. He might gain in income, earn praise for his enterprise, but at the cost of losing the gentle, relaxed atmosphere that surrounds this oasis of long-established farming methods.

There is only one farm now. Walter amalgamated with Jack, while Bill Trevorrow sold his land but kept the farmhouse for his daughter Mary and her husband Mike, and built a bungalow a few hundred yards away where he lives alone now that Cath, his wife, has died. Cath was renowned for her cooking and the way she looked after holiday visitors, and it was from Bill that we bought Oliver land where stands the Ambrose Rock.

We see Meg, his brown and white spaniel, more often than we see Bill. Meg is bone receiver-in-chief, and if we have only one bone to dispose of she receives priority over Trigger and one-eyed Whisky. She is very well mannered and after receiving the bone she will wag her tail, hurry with bone in mouth to the iron-bar gate in front of the bungalow, struggle, because she is a plump lady, through the gap between two bars and then will turn round to look at us again, plainly saying thank you. It is easy to understand, therefore, how embarrassed we are when we see Meg and we have no bone; and why it is that, on such an occasion, I may stop the car, get out and apologise.

I stop the car, too, when I see Bill in the lane, and we have one of those desultory conversations like I have with Walter. I saw him one morning after it had been announced that there was a glut of eggs and that producers were going bankrupt.

'I tell you what,' he said, wearing a cap that you see American soldiers wear, and which I presumed he had acquired during a trip to America to visit his brother, 'people see that eggs and poultry are making good money so they move in to do likewise, but there are soon too many and the prices drop. Same with pigs, same with beef cattle, same with cows. A good living when there are a few but hopeless when there are too many. Look at bulbs and you know this as well as I do. There was a good living to make out of daffodils once, but the big fellows moved in on them and that was the end of the small grower getting a fair price.'

I agreed with him, and I added there was another aspect to this theme appertaining to Cornwall. Once there were relatively few hotels scattered around Cornwall and they did well because they catered for people who came on holiday to enjoy the tranquil qualities of Cornwall. Then more and more hotels were opened up until there were too many, and this resulted in a cry from the hoteliers that more should be done to attract tourists in the manner that Butlins attracted their crowds. Certain holiday areas, like Newquay, already attracted such crowds, but those who loved Cornwall for tranquil holidays did not want a Newquay in other parts of Cornwall, and they never will. Those, for instance, who seek to turn our own West Cornwall, the wildest and hitherto the most unspoilt part of Cornwall, into a raucous holiday area, will destroy themselves. This beautiful area in which we live is for the sensitive. It is no place for crowds.

Until recently Walter and Jack had a dairy herd and they provided us with our milk. Whenever we required it, we used to leave a large milk can outside Jack's house, he would fill it when milking was done and later we would go up and fetch it. Then on our return to the cottage, Jeannie would pour the milk into a large pan, let it stand for a few hours until the cream came to the top, then simmer it on low heat until it became clotted.

This happens no more. Jack is no longer a dairy farmer and instead he specialises in young beef cattle. This has meant the end of our enjoyment of Cornish clotted cream because such old-fashioned Cornish cream is no longer available anywhere. It has something to do with health regulations. The bureaucrats decreed that milk straight from the cow and turned into cream was a health risk, hence the ban. Hence the factory-made Cornish cream of today which has no similarity to the Cornish cream of old.

Fred and Merlin miss Jack's cows. Fred used to enjoy his conversations with one of them, Fred one side of the hedge, the cow the other side. They would stare solemnly at each other for half an hour at a time, and sometimes they would be joined by Merlin; and the three of them would continue their mysterious discussion.

157

Bullocks, however, are not so amiable, especially when they are young and have moved to new pastures. Then they can behave like a teenage gang, and their leader will nose around looking for a weakness in the new pasture's defences. Once it has found a weakness it will barge through it and the rest will follow in a stampede.

Jack was aware of this, of course, and he was apprehensive as to how the young bullocks would behave when they were in the fields near our cottage, for Jack was one of those people who, though tough in his fight for survival, willing to work eighty, ninety hours a week, was considerate of others. That has been part of the charm of being part of this farming oasis a mile away from the main road... without being forced to co-operate, we do.

Thus, when on those occasions Jack's young bullocks have found a gap in the defences and then stampeded into Minack country, threatening all possible kinds of damage, my reaction has not been one of anger, but of a subconscious pleasure that I had now the opportunity of responding to the comradeship in our oasis.

Fred and Merlin, however, did not share my view. Harmless gossiping with a Guernsey cow was now a memory. Instead they ran the risk of confrontation with thirty or forty aggro-minded bullocks, and quite soon after Jack had become a beef-cattle farmer, Fred and Merlin had such a confrontation.

Jeannie and I had been to Penzance, taking several chips of tomatoes to our wholesaler. We had only been away an hour, but when we returned, as soon as the car drew up, I heard that special trumpeting hee-haw that comes from Fred when something has upset him greatly. I hurried up to the field above the cottage where we had left the two of them, and found twenty or more bullocks circling the field at speed while Fred was standing at bay, his back to the wood, with one bullock larger than the others advancing

158

upon him, head down, menacingly. But where was Merlin?

Jeannie arrived with a stick and she stood beside Fred brandishing it like a lady warrior beside her faithful steed, while I ran through the gap at the far end of the field into the wood meadow calling: 'Merlin! Merlin!' Then into the wood I went: 'Merlin! Merlin!' No sign of him.

As always when the bullocks were on the rampage, we had to get the news to Jack as soon as possible so that he could come and restore order; and this we were intending to do after I had traced the whereabouts of Merlin. Poor Merlin.

Merlin had panicked. Unlike Fred, who had stood his ground, Merlin had fled when he saw the bullock invasion. He had leapt two bars which blocked a gap in the field which led first to Jeannie's washing line, then to the Lama field, and once there his terror was such that he rushed to a tiny gap with barbed wire across it which lead to the QE2 field. It was there that I found him. A bewildered, trembling

donkey with a cut on his nose, and I was amazed that he had escaped so lightly.

A few hours later, fences mended, bullocks back where they should have been, Jack appeared with a large bag.

He smiled at me.

'Conscience carrots,' he said, and I laughed when he added: 'The bullocks apologise.'

ELEVEN

I first heard the yelping of the hounds while I was waiting by the tap of the one-time china sink in the donkey field. I had to wait by the tap as it filled the sink because, as had happened several times before, if I go away I forget it is running; and if it goes on running long enough, the well, whence comes the water, goes dry.

Thus I was standing there when away in the direction of Jack's farmhouse, I heard this yelping, coming nearer and nearer.

It was a calm day, so calm that I could have believed it was a September day instead of a day of early winter. It was 'a day lent', as the Cornish say. And in the calmness came this sound, louder and louder, of yelping hounds.

Jeannie appeared. She was wearing mottled-grey close-fitting trousers and a polo-neck jersey.

'Shut that tap off,' she called out, 'It's the hunt. They're after one of our foxes of the Brontë wood!'

Now I could see the riders silhouetted against the skyline, a scattering of riders, some plunging into Jack's kale field, others galloping across the field above the clover field. There was the banshee cry of a hunting horn and then I saw the pink coat of the huntsman, the yelping hounds ahead of him, and they were about to reach the gate which opened to a track which led to our lane. Once they reached the lane they would be able to storm down to the clover field, across to the Clarence meadow, and to the Brontë wood. I thought back to June days when we had seen the cubs at play, and the vixen watching.

'Where are you going?'

It was a silly question to ask: it was obvious where Jeannie was going. She was setting off up the lane to meet the hounds.

'You better stay with the donkeys,' she called back, 'in case the hounds change direction.'

The donkeys, ears pricked, Fred snorting, were enjoying themselves, an exciting diversion to their day. But in the next field, Jack's bullocks were careering round and round as if in a panic.

'Be careful, Jeannie,' I shouted.

I knew, of course, that my advice would not be heeded. Jeannie was one of those people who is unafraid once a course has been decided upon. Indeed, in my imagination I sometimes concern myself as to her reaction in certain circumstances. For instance, in a corner of the sitting-room she keeps her father's sword. Her father, Frank Nicol, was in the London Scottish during the First World War and the sword was part of his equipment. When he died it came into Jeannie's possession, and although it is sheathed, there are volatile moments when she might use it.

One such occasion would be if she discovered an intruder in the cottage. She says she would poise the sword in front of him, threatening to pierce him – and I have had frequently to explain to her that if such a situation materialised and she carried out the act, I would for a long time be making a weekly visit to one of Her Majesty's prisons. The fact that she was defending her home would not count. Governments could excuse their actions by saying that attacking a country was in fact a defence of their own, but such an excuse has no validity for the householder. He is the villain if he defends his property.

Another occasion when she threatens she would make use of the sword, a much more likely one, is if sadistic vandals attacked the donkeys... or Ambrose. Heaven knows what would happen to the vandals if they did so. I believe, and it is my worry plus admiration, that nothing would stop her from unsheathing the sword and advancing upon them.

She had gone up the lane and she was no longer in sight. I decided to check the whereabouts of Ambrose and I found him, as I expected, lying in the hay in the Orlyt. He was alert, and no wonder, he could easily hear the yelping hounds. But he was safe there on the hay after I had shut the door.

I went back to the donkeys, and the yelping continued to come nearer, and the donkeys became more excited, and the bullocks continued to race round the neighbouring field. I suddenly remembered an overnight visit Jeannie and I had made five years before to Alfoxton, once the home of Wordsworth, in the Quantock Hills of Somerset.

We had left our hotel in the morning and set off on one of those lovely walks that release you from all tensions. Our route lay across a stretch of moorland covered with heather which was so bare of trees and bushes on either side of the track that we both remarked on it. It was like a grouse moor in Scotland.

We had gone some distance when we saw a figure ahead of us, perhaps six hundred yards away. I was carrying my fieldglasses so I looked through them at the figure and saw that it was a small, elderly man who was wearing a strangely cut jacket, an equally strange hat and knee breeches. I handed the fieldglasses to Jeannie and she remarked also on his unusual appearance. We realised we would come face to face with him in a few minutes and we continued to walk. We both, as it happened, had our heads down.

The few minutes went by and we met no one.

'Where on earth has that man got to?' I said.

We looked on either side of the track, looking across the bare moorland, and there was not a sign of him. There was no possibility of him having hidden because there was no cover. He had just vanished.

We recounted our experience when we returned to the hotel. A local was there, and after we had finished, he stared at us as if we were two people from outer space. Then he said: 'You've seen the ghost of the Dog Pound!'

I had always thought you only saw ghosts at night, never in broad daylight. Indeed I am still subconsciously sceptical that we saw the man. But Jeannie saw him too, and I don't suppose both of us could have imagined him. Anyhow the local told us the story of the ghost of the Dog Pound.

Close by to where we had been walking, the hounds of the local hunt, many years ago, were kenneled in this place called the Dog Pound. The huntsman in charge of them used to mingle with them every day wearing his pink coat (I have never understood why in hunting parlance it is called pink, when it is so plainly red) and then one day he went to the Dog Pound in his everyday clothes, and the hounds didn't recognise him... and they tore him to pieces. The ghost of the Dog Pound has haunted the area ever since. A gruesome tale, and for Jeannie and me, a puzzling one.

Jeannie had been away for twenty minutes and I would have been worried about her had I not seen the huntsman again, and the hounds, and members of the hunt galloping across another of Jack's fields, but this time going westwards away from us. None the less I was impatient to learn what had happened after she had gone up the lane. I was soon to know. Jeannie arrived back exuding an aura of indignation.

'I reached the well,' she said (this was the well we use in summer), 'and the whole pack of hounds were rushing towards me. I shouted and shouted at the huntsman behind them and he called them to stop... and it was amazing how they obeyed him. Then I saw a lady on a black horse in the Actaea field, and she was trying to make the horse jump over the hedge into the lane, and he wouldn't do it. So she called out to me, asking how she could get out of the field. I said "get out of it the way you came in," wherever that might have been. Then I went up to find Jack, but the door of the house was locked, and while I was standing there all sorts of riders appeared, not Vogue-type riders but ratcatcher-type riders . . . and I told them what I thought of them, and told them never to come this way again.'

Jeannie paused. There was an apologetic note in her voice.

'They didn't know who I was. They might think I was Alice.'

Alice was Jack's wife, and a special friend.

'Heavens,' I said, 'Alice would have been proud of you.'

And she was; Jack too. They had taken a rare day off.

There is a postscript to this incident. Ten minutes after Jeannie had returned we decided to take the donkeys up to the clover field. We reached the gate at the corner of the lane and were met by the pungent scent of a fox. He had made it. While Jeannie was facing the hounds, the fox had had time to run through the undergrowth, then over the hedge by the gate, across the clover field and the Clarence meadow to the Brontë wood and the cliff.

All through November I was clearing the daffodil fields and meadows of grass and undergrowth. The task is divided into two sections. One section, and the easiest section, is where the land is flat and accessible, for then I use the Condor which devours up grass and undergrowth at a pace. It is, however, physically exhausting because holding the handle-bars as it roars across a field is like riding a horse in a rodeo. But at least the task is straightforward and results are quickly achieved. 'Have you finished already?' Jeannie will ask after I have roared round the California field.

The second section is a more intimate task. This is when I use the Japanese Brush Cutter to clear the daffodil meadows which fall down the cliff to the sea's edge in the manner of an Italian vineyard. Each meadow is very small. Each meadow was created long before the birth of modern farming, long before economists exposed the foolishness of believing pride in goods supplied. When we first came to Minack, for instance, the first new potatoes were treated with the reverence sophisticated gardeners reserve for orchids. There was always rivalry between the cliff potato growers as to who would be the first to send to market, but there was never any cheating. The first new potatoes had always to be perfect in size and condition. They would be soil clean when they were placed in what was called a chip, green leaves of the potato plant lining the chip to soften friction during travel; and when these chips had been carried up the cliff, weighed and labelled, one felt a glow of achievement. Often the final work was done on early May mornings when there was a haze over the sea, and swallows would be flying in from the west, and there were all the distilling scents of a summer's beginning.

When I set off with the brush cutter to the cliff meadows, I always suffered from being controlled by Pisces, my birth sign. I always argue with myself as to which of the meadows I should begin cutting. I will wake up in the morning and say to Jeannie that I am going to cut the far meadows, then change my mind after breakfast, saying I am going down Minack cliff which meant I was going to cut the meadows which, with Tommy Williams, our eccentric, devoted, first helper, we first carved out of the untamed land that was to give us a livelihood. Once when he was pausing from digging up the potatoes, I saw him leaning on his long-handle Cornish shovel and heard him saying as if to himself as he stared out to sea: 'What more can a man want than a morning like this and a view like that?'

I move into a small meadow on a steep slope, the brush cutter slung across my shoulder, and begin weaving it to and fro like a scythe, the circular blade spinning at speed, the two-stroke engine roaring with a noise like that of a motorbike. I know every meadow so intimately that I will be aware that under one layer of bracken lies a clump of pink campion that flowers all through the winter, and so I will attack the bracken very delicately and save the pink campion. Violets also abound in these cliff meadows and I am always on the watch for them; and if by mistake I lop one off, I curse myself for doing so. I have to keep a look out, also, for an early primrose, and if I find a clump, I will switch off the brush cutter, lay it on the ground, then bend down to the clump and bury my face in the petals. When one is unobserved, one can behave at such moments in a very basic fashion.

At the bottom of the Minack cliff, just above the last of our daffodil meadows, a meadow poised just above the sea so that you lean over the hedge at one end and stare down at water, was once a thriving palm tree. The trunk of it still stands there, a forlorn sight, but we will never cut it down.

For it is, in a way, a memorial. The palm tree died in that ferocious Saturday-night storm which caused the Mousehole lifeboat and *Union Star* disaster.

On the Sunday before this disaster Jeannie and I had a strange experience. During the course of the previous twelve months we had a tame rook we called Ron who regularly visited us, perching on the roof, waiting for us to throw a piece of bread. Often it would follow us when we went for a walk, flying from one spot to another, settling for a moment on a hawthorn branch then following us as we walked onwards. We became very fond of him.

On the Sunday, I drove on my own to Penzance to collect the papers and when I came back, after I had crossed Monty's Leap, I was met by a running Jeannie, running down the path past the cottage towards me. Something obviously had perturbed her, and so, instead of driving the car into the garage, I jammed on the brakes when I was opposite the barn. The story she had to tell me was extraordinary.

We keep our two dustbins in a gap just outside the wooden building once known as the apple house, but now christened the cat's kitchen because it is there on a discarded calor gas stove that Jeannie boils the coley for Ambrose.

'I've had a terrible shock,' she said, and Jeannie is not the sort of person who fakes emotion, 'I think Ron is dead. Come and have a look. I don't understand because it doesn't look like him...'

It is on such occasions that one becomes sceptical of the judgment of those who depend on reason to justify their judgments. For reason, I am sure, had no explanation for what occurred that Sunday morning, and for what, some people may say, it foreshadowed.

Jeannie had taken a bowl of kitchen refuse down to one of the dustbins, had lifted the lid and dropped the contents inside, and had taken a few steps on her way back to the cottage when there was a gentle thud behind her. She looked back and saw on the ground, alongside the dustbin, quite still, a bird the size of a rook. At that moment she was certain it was Ron.

Doubt set in when she saw that there was no dark grey about its beak, and also because earlier in the day Ron had been on the roof and she had thrown him a slice of bread. She could not believe, therefore, that Ron was lying there dead and she waited anxiously for my return, waiting hopefully my confirmation that it was not Ron.

I had one look at the feathered body by the dustbin and reassured her that it was not. Ron, I suggested, had taken his slice of bread and flown away, pleased as usual that we had fed him. The dead bird Jeannie thought was Ron, I explained to her, was not a rook but a carrion crow. I had noticed this carrion crow during the previous few days.

I had noticed it because it had regularly taken up a position on the branches of the elm trees that surround the apple house (or cat's kitchen) and small greenhouse. They were dying elm trees and if a bird took up a stance on a branch, it was easily seen. I had seen this carrion crow sitting on a bare branch for hour after hour, as if it was waiting for something. I hate carrion crows because in springtime they will destroy every nest in their neighbourhood, but I did nothing to shoo this one away. I do not understand why. I suppose the sight of it had become familiar and it had become, therefore, part of the scene; and now it was dead I felt sorry. At the same time I felt an indefinable sense of doom. It had died so suddenly, so strangely, dropping like that almost at Jeannie's feet. The superstitious side of me had become involved. I looked down at the still-shiny black feathers and felt apprehensive.

A few minutes later we walked back to the cottage and as we did so Ron appeared from the direction of Lamorna,

made a circle over the wood, then floated down on to the roof.

'There's Ron,' I said cheerfully to Jeannie, 'so you don't have to worry about him.'

I went into the kitchen, picked up a slice of bread, went outside again and threw the piece up on the roof. Ron slid down on his backside, seized it in his beak and flew off. All very normal. He had behaved like this off and on for months, usually every day, though sometimes he would disappear for a week or two. This time, after Jeannie's shock, we were particularly pleased to see him. Yet, as I will tell, there was another strange outcome to this Sunday, six days before the Mousehole tragedy.

Meanwhile, as I cut down the grass and undergrowth of the meadow below the desolate palm tree, I continued to reflect on the circumstances of that Saturday night.

I remember that Jeannie and I had a late supper.

Usually it was about half past seven, but this time it was after eight. Normally Ambrose was in the cottage by then, but on this occasion there was no sign of him. We were not concerned. He was always a bit wild when a gale blew, and time and time again Jeannie had said to me: 'We must get Ambrose in before the gale gets too bad.' It seems that he loves gales. He has a marvellous sense of adventure when the wind rushes through the bushes and hisses through the trees while he hides listening to our calls, ignoring them.

We ourselves proceeded to have a normal evening. After

supper I settled down on the sofa to read a book, Roger Venables *Portrait of D*, I think it was (D was a famous Oxford don), while Jeannie was amusing herself reading Jennifer's Diary in *Harper's Bazaar*. Jennifer is the cover name of Betty Kenward whom Jeannie knew when she was at the Savoy. Betty Kenward began humbly with a freelance contribution to a magazine, a gossip paragraph, and she progressed via the *Tatler* to be the most-read Society diarist in the world. She has the most extraordinary memory. She takes no notes. She will go to a party, know and remember everyone who is present and a ream of names will in due course appear in the Diary. It is a feat of memory which bewilders people. One evening, on one of our visits to London, we had drinks with her: and listening to her recounting the stories of Society over the past fifty years was as if I was listening to Proust describing the world of Oriane Guermantes, Robert St Loup and Baron de Charlus.

I do not remember the exact time I put down my book and switched on the TV. I wish I did. I did not even remember exactly when it was next morning ... next morning when we were woken up at six by the headlights of cars coming down the lane, cars with ITV and BBC television crews, the moment when we learnt of the disaster that had taken place barely half a mile away. For what I want to know is this: did I hear the engine of the lifeboat *before* she reached the *Union Star*, or after she had crashed against the vessel, then going round and round out of control before sinking?

What I do remember is this. The two Ronnies were on BBC 1 that night, but their programme instead of ending at 9 pm was scheduled to end ten minutes later. I had been ready to listen to the News but as it was not 9 pm, I switched to ITV. Nothing there we wanted to watch. Nothing either on BBC 2. Somewhere around this time, and this is the puzzle, I went to our bedroom window and began calling for Ambrose. It did not take long for him to appear and as I saw him coming towards me, I heard the scream of an engine out to sea. Ambrose jumped up on the window ledge and I picked him up and shut the window. Then I went back into the sitting-room and said to Jeannie: 'A boat out there is having a struggle to get back to Newlyn.' Obviously, from the sound of the engine, I thought the boat was going eastwards. The drama, however, was taking place to the west.

I completed cutting down the meadow below the forlorn palm tree and decided to take a rest, undoing the harness of the brush cutter and sitting down on a rock overlooking the sea. My mind continued to wonder about that disastrous night.

The last radio contact with the lifeboat, the official inquiry in due course confirmed, was at 9.21. Nothing more was known of her until around midnight when wreckage began coming in at Lamorna Cove. A news vacuum of two hours and a half.

Did I therefore hear her last dying moments as she circled out of control a mile, perhaps, off our bay? Wreckage came into our bay which would seem to confirm this. Or was it the sound of the lifeboat on her fateful way to the *Union Star*? The scream of the engine that night will always haunt me.

As I said, there was another strange outcome to that Sunday six days before the disaster, when the carrion crow dropped dead close to Jeannie.

We never saw Ron again.

TWELVE

We pinned most of our Christmas cards, as always, along the wooden beams of the sitting-room. After supper on Christmas Eve we were sipping sloe gin, me on the sofa, Jeannie with Ambrose on her lap in the armchair in front of the fire, when Jeannie said: 'Think of the goodwill which prompted people to send those cards. Think of the goodwill like this that is taking place in millions of homes.'

'You've got the Christmas spirit.'

'Yes, I have. There is a surge of it all over this country, over many parts of the world. Why does it only have to last a day?'

'Jeannie, I will tell you.'

A finger was stroking the top of Ambrose's head.

'Are you laughing at me? Are you thinking that I am being sentimental just because it is Christmas?'

'No, of course not. Some people would say your remark was so obvious it was not worth saying. Yet it is a profound truth. Unfortunately in this cynical age, profound truths are often dismissed as being banal, because they have been said often before. That doesn't stop them from being profound truths.'

'Why, why is it then that the people of the world want to destroy each other, always want to fight each other in some corner of the world?'

'It's my theory that around two thousand people are responsible, probably much less.'

'How do you mean?'

'Well,' I said, 'ordinary people never want war. Maybe they can be provoked into wanting it, but it is obvious that they would much prefer to go about their daily business. Who, then, does the provoking? I'm saying they belong to a group of ambitious leaders. Supposing I say there are twenty such leaders, and each leader in his country has a hundred obedient acolytes, that adds up to two thousand people who do not mind bringing misery to their fellow human beings.'

A small log fell out of the fire, and there was an aroma of woodsmoke.

'I see your point. It's frightening. Only two thousand people, and they can ruin the world. But what can be done about them?'

I laughed.

'What is needed,' I said, 'is a sort of James Bond with a hit list!'

'They are not the only people who are ruining the world,' said Jeannie, 'think of the scientists who are responsible for the acid rain which is destroying the forests of Germany.'

A German friend had written to us saying that a forester in the Black Forest went away for a fortnight's holiday, and when he returned he didn't recognise the area in which he had been working.

'Mad!' said Jeannie, 'they're all mad!'

'Yes,' I said, 'brilliant minds have gone mad.'

'All over the world,' went on Jeannie, 'scientists are creating chemicals and weapons of destruction. They test them in laboratories, declare them safe and then years later admit they were wrong. Huge vested interests backing them, governments backing them too.'

'Governments have reasons for backing them.'

'What reasons?'

'Factories. Source of employment.'

I find it wearisome when spokesmen of any political party

174

declare, as an excuse for any unpleasantness or hardship the public has to endure, that the sacrifice is 'for our children's future'. I have heard this phrase *ad nauseam* during my lifetime. It is a phrase that has echoed down the ages, generation after generation, the winning post always lying just ahead of the next generation. A relay race that never ends. Even weapons of destruction are explained away as being necessary 'for our children's future'.

Ambrose jumped down from Jeannie's lap and made for the door, wanting to be let out. I looked at my watch, soon it would be time for the Christmas Eve custom of giving mincepies to the donkeys. 'Wait a moment, Ambrose,' I said, not wanting to be interrupted.

'I read of a chilling theory the other day,' I went on, 'the writer was dealing with the massive overpopulation in many parts of this planet and he was pointing out that nature counters overpopulation among animals by culling them through disease. Then he went on to say that nature, or whatever you like to call this superior power, is setting out to treat the human race in the same kind of way. All these horrific chemicals and weapons of destruction are being created to keep the population on this planet within liveable control. After all,' I said, adding my own point of view, 'if population growth continues at the present rate, it will be like putting a thousand people in a ten foot square room.'

The clock, the clock that the directors of the Savoy Hotel gave Jeannie when she left to come to Minack, struck ten.

'Come on,' said Jeannie, 'let's go to the donkeys.'

For a long time we used to take mincepies to Penny and Fred at a quarter to midnight, then after ten minutes we would leave them, because we had been told by an old man who had lived his life with donkeys that they always knelt on the stroke of midnight; and so we left them, five minutes before, because we did not want to be disillusioned. If they knelt, let them do so unwatched.

Penny, Fred's mother, died a few days after one Christmas. On that particular Christmas Eve Jeannie had carried the customary mincepies on a plate to the stables while I, on arrival there, had lit the candle which we kept, all the year round, in the candlestick placed on the ledge of the stable window. On lighting it that Christmas Eve the candle flared up then collapsed into a waxy pool. I felt a chill go through me as it did so; I knew then that Penny was soon to die. Thus it is, as a memory to her, that we have left the candlestick on the ledge of the stable window. No candle. Just the wax of that Christmas Eve a few days before Penny, a donkey who came from the Connemara hills to Minack, died.

Merlin, shaggy Merlin, hootless Merlin, had only been with us a couple of months before he received his initiation to the mincepie custom. The initiation was a disaster. There we were, Jeannie and I, still maintaining the tradition of mincepies at a quarter to midnight... but when Jeannie offered him a mincepie, he spat it out on to the stable floor. It was after this incident that we decided, instead of keeping awake for the midnight occasion, that we would perform it earlier. The following Christmas Eve we were apprehensive. Would Merlin behave in the same way again? Jeannie offered him a mincepie, and he gobbled it.

We found them this time standing side-by-side in the stable, Fred snuffling at the sight of us, Merlin silent. Merlin had gone lame a week before. I found him one morning standing immobile in the field. When I put a halter on him and tried to persuade him to move, he hobbled a few steps, then stopped. He was in great pain.

We soon had the vet out to see him and the vet found that pebbles had lodged in the hoof of his left foreleg and they had formed an abscess. The vet proceeded to clean the hoof, using a penknife, and it would have been understandable if Merlin had reacted like a rodeo donkey. Instead, as I

held him on the halter, he remained quite still. A gentle patient. Then the vet squirted a blue-coloured medicine into the hoof, saying that the hoof had now to be kept dry and clean. There was only one way to achieve this. Merlin had to wear a sock, one of my socks. Merlin, however, discarded after a few hours first one sock then another, and they would be left in some corner of the field. I was to lose three pairs of socks in this way.

I had placed the torch on the ledge of the window beside the candlestick, and the torch shone on the limewashed wall opposite. The donkeys, as they munched their mincepies, and ourselves were in shadow. So too the end of the stables where there were two shelves spaced above each other, reaching from one side of the stables to the other. On the top shelf were six large boxes, the contents of which had recently placed me in a dilemma.

The contents consisted of twenty-four thousand polythene bags each decorated by a colourful design of a map of Cornwall in yellow, a spray of daffodils and the slogan A LAMORNA PACK. The bags dated back to a time when Jeannie and I thought we were going to make a fortune by selling our bulbs in packs. So hopeful were we that we ordered twenty-five thousand of the packs... and we still had the twenty-four thousand left. Left because as soon as we had started our venture, big growers moved in and we could not compete.

However, the chance had come this summer to dispose of them, and we were thereupon faced by this dilemma which people often have to face. What price has integrity? Everyone has a price, a city gentleman said to me recently. Then asked: 'What's yours?'

The chance came when we were visited by one of the most distinguished distributors of bulbs in the country, a man of charm and enthusiasm. I showed him one of the bags and his reaction was immediate. He thought it a wonderfully designed bag (Jeannie had been the designer) and I watched him staring at it for a couple of minutes, and holding it up to the light. Then he made a remark which startled me.

'I'll give you £2,000 for those twenty-four thousand bags,' he said, 'I have my chequebook with me. I'll write out the cheque straightaway if you agree.'

There was, however, a line, an indelible line, on the Lamorna Pack, which separated us from the £2,000. The line read 'Packed by Tangye, St Buryan', and such a line could have given a false impression. My bulb distributor friend understood and the offer was withdrawn.

When Christmas is over and the New Year, a restful time begins at Minack. We are waiting for the daffodils, we have time on our own, and in January Cornwall belongs to its residents and for them it becomes like a huge garden. Roads are free of drivers who think they are still on motorways, carparks are free of attendants, beaches are empty for gulls and other seabirds, one can walk for miles on the coastal path without seeing anyone coming towards one, and while one reads accounts of a harsh winter elsewhere, one rejoices in the dawning of spring. Courting ravens grunt at each other, coltsfoot perfumes the bank of a stream, a sudden primrose shines in a meadow and spikes of early daffodils show above ground. One is aware that the world is beginning again, not the Man-made world but the world of Creation. It is a slow world which one watches. One has to have patience to see it, and feel it. It is the feeling of it which enriches the soul. Anyone can *see* the countryside. The lucky ones are those who have the time to be absorbed by it.

I could not, however, have been a countryman all my life. I had to experience the city life of rushing for trains, queuing for buses, being anxious about my job and, for that matter, living at times a life of elegant sophistication. Jeannie and I had done all these things and, like so many others, there arrived a moment in our lives when we knew we had to break away.

We still return though, still from time to time experience again the life we have left. We enjoy ourselves, but part of that enjoyment is the knowledge that we will only be away for three or four days. Indeed it is my custom to say to Jeannie when we set off for London, luggage in the back of the Volvo, slowly going over Monty's Leap, then on up the winding lane... it is my custom to say to Jeannie: 'Now that we have started, we are already on the way back here!'

We were, for instance, already planning a visit to London in a few weeks time to coincide with the publication date of Jeannie's *Bertioni's Hotel*. It was not an occasion to treat casually. It had taken five years to write, five years during which she kept much of her planning and plotting secret. She did not discuss the story with me. She would lie awake at night wrestling with the story problems, go for walks on her own and disappear in her hut with a window that looks out onto Mounts Bay, and write. She had many interruptions, many times when her involvement in the novel was fractured. So publication time was not to be treated casually.

At the end of January she had received a couple of advance copies, one of which she sent to Beverley Nichols. She had shared with Beverley several cat-worshipping sessions which one-time cat haters like myself abhor. I am now a convert, true enough, but I still disapprove of the fawning, embarrassing way that cat worshippers sometimes behave. I was at a loss, for instance, when one day I was taking Beverley and Jeannie around the Lands End area when they suddenly called me to stop because they had seen a large tortoiseshell cat on the windowsill of a cottage and they wanted to talk to it.

The last time we saw Beverley was in the previous September. He had always had connections with West Cornwall: he used to go to Sennen Cove as a child before the First World War; and in the sixties his brother was a vicar, first of Sancreed, then of Sennen. It was when his brother was at Sancreed that we first had contact with him. He had praised the first of the Minack Chronicles, *A Gull on the Roof*, in a magazine and I heard by chance, after reading the article, that he was staying with his brother at Sancreed. So, as it was daffodil time, Jeannie and I gathered together a huge collection of daffodils and hastened to the vicarage to thank him for what he had done for us. We were too late. He had returned to London and it was not until a couple of years later that we met him, and our friendship began.

That September, that previous September, he had come to stay for two days at the Queen's Hotel in Penzance and we were with him each day. The first day he came to lunch at Minack and, in cat-worshipping fashion, tried to woo Ambrose. He failed. Ambrose has never been the victim of flattery. Indeed it is odd how Beverley who, after all, created the immortal description of people who are F or non-F, was never able to cope with the eccentricities of the cats at Minack.

180

The first encounter was with Lama, the little black cat who came to us in a storm. Beverley had come to lunch one day, wanted a rest afterwards and asked Lama if she would share the rest with him. In fact it was not a question of asking: Lama was picked up and carried to the spare room. Ten minutes later the spare room door was edged open, and Lama darted back into the sitting-room. 'They've had words,' Jeannie said.

Another occasion was when Oliver was courting us. Oliver, also a black cat, who had decided to make a home with us at the ending stage of Lama's life, and who, one October morning, produced from the undergrowth near Monty's Leap the tiny, autumn-bracken-coloured kitten, which was the double of Monty and who is Ambrose. But before Ambrose appeared, the previous Christmas in fact, and when Oliver was spending his nights in a little house I had made for him in the undergrowth, Beverley and Jeannie tried to lure him out of his undergrowth house towards a plate of turkey. Oliver ignored their blandishments.

After lunch that first day we went to Sennen Cove and he stood outside the Victorian built cottage that looked out on the sweep of the bay towards Cape Cornwall, and where he had spent his holidays as a child. It was called Nile Cottage and Jeannie persuaded him to stand by it so she could take a photograph. Nearby was a steep sand dune, now removed, but when Beverley came there as a child he told us that one of his chief memories was sliding down it on a metal tray, like a toboggan. There we were then, with this man who was believed to have the most brilliant future of any of his generation: president of the Oxford Union, hailed by the critics for his books in his early twenties, very good looking, a musician, a friend of the famous of his day. Suddenly, as we stood outside Nile Cottage, he became emotional and asked us to take him back to his hotel. What was going through his mind? He was once a golden boy with such a shining future of brilliance ahead of him, and then somewhere along the years it faltered. His last book, an autobiography, is called *The Unforgiving Minute*. What was that minute? I will always regret that I never asked him. But his epitaph is this: He gave much pleasure to many people.

One of the endearing features of Beverley was his letter-writing. His letters were short, often witty, always full of feeling; and it was one such letter that Jeannie received from him after she had sent him that early copy of *Bertioni's Hotel*. It read:

> *Your book is a real achievement ... strangely moving, and technically far more brilliant than you have done before. I was deeply impressed by the steady build-up of detail. One felt the very essence of the vast complex of the hotel ... the actual smell and shape of it. And your characters are fascinating in their every movement.*

Unlike the previous year, the daffodils were early this year and by Valentine's Day we were busy picking the cliff meadows. On the morning of Valentine's Day we went picking before breakfast and the chosen meadow was the one at the bottom of the cliff, a flat meadow, poised twenty or thirty feet above the sea.

There had been a southerly gale during the previous two days, but during the night it had veered to the west. It was still blowing strongly and when I took the dust from our fireplace down to the dustbin, it blew back at me and specks, for a moment, hurt my eyes.

When, however, Jeannie and I reached the cliff meadows it was as still as if we had been in a South Sea lagoon. It was another world. Up in the fields a gale, but down the cliff this stillness. We were glad that the wind had veered to the west. But the sea remained menacing. When the gale roared from the south the fury of the sea was easy to observe: great rollers, great chasms between them, rushed at angles to our cliff, exploded in a Guy Fawkes display of spray. Not so that morning of Valentine's Day after the wind had veered to the west.

The sea, that morning when we took our wicker daffodil baskets down to our bottom meadow, appeared calm. It

was the calmness of a rolling, undulating plain. Stormy, yes, and grey, and yet, because of the wind veering to the west, the impression was that the southerly gales of the previous two days no longer mattered.

Then, as we began to pick, each of us bent double, Jeannie much faster than me, pick, pick, pick . . . we would straighten our backs, give ourselves a pause, look out to sea. And looking we would suddenly watch how the sheltered sea, sheltered by the change in direction of the wind to the west, had remained enraged. Out of that calm, undulating sea huge killer waves suddenly drove towards the rocks beneath the daffodil meadow where we were picking, and exploded.

At last our two baskets were full, both very heavy, even one on its own far too heavy for Jeannie to carry. So I began the weary way up the tortuous path of the cliff with a basket in either hand, Jeannie following behind me, watching for daffodil stems that might fall out of the baskets as I clambered.

We had just reached the cottage, hungry for breakfast, when the little red Post Office van arrived down the lane with our post.

Valentine's Day. Last year Ambrose had one. Jeannie and I had none.

This particular morning the postman delivered three letters. One was a bill. Of the other two, one was addressed to Jeannie, the other addressed to me.

'Jeannie,' I said, doubtfully, after opening mine, reading what it said, 'did you send this?'

She looked at me with amusement.

'Didn't you say last year that a Valentine Card was a weapon of mystery?'

ANN DRYSDALE

FAINT HEART NEVER KISSED A PIG

is the unforgettable tale of adorable Ernest, the burglar-proof porker; Snuff, the blackest sheep you ever saw, who arrived at Hagg House just one hour old, shivering and wet; and Dodo, the indescribably ugly guinea fowl . . .

It is the enchanting tale of one remarkable woman, Ann Drysdale, who, with her three children, left the civilised world of London and a career in journalism, to set up home in a North Yorkshire hill farm.

And how, amidst great hardship and even greater hilarity, the Drysdales and their extended family made out . . .

AUTOBIOGRAPHY   0 7221 3070 8   £1.75

A selection of bestsellers from SPHERE

FICTION

VITAL SIGNS	Barbara Wood	£2.95 ☐
THE ZURICH NUMBERS	Bill Granger	£2.75 ☐
NOCTURNE FOR THE GENERAL	John Trenhaile	£2.50 ☐
HOTEL DE LUXE	Caroline Gray	£2.95 ☐

FILM & TV TIE-INS

BOON	Anthony Masters	£2.50 ☐
LADY JANE	Anthony Smith	£1.95 ☐

NON-FICTION

LIVING WITH DOGS	Sheila Hocken	£3.50 ☐
FIT OR FAT TARGET DIET	Covert Bailey	£2.50 ☐
MORE LOVE SEX AND ASTROLOGY	Teri King	£2.50 ☐
THE CYNIC'S LEXICON	Jonathon Green	£3.95 ☐

All Sphere books are available at your local bookshop or newsagent, or can be ordered direct from the publisher. Just tick the titles you want and fill in the form below.

Name _____

Address _____

_____

Write to Sphere Books, Cash Sales Department, P.O. Box 11, Falmouth, Cornwall TR10 9EN

Please enclose a cheque or postal order to the value of the cover price plus:

UK: 55p for the first book, 22p for the second book and 14p for each additional book ordered to a maximum charge of £1.75.

OVERSEAS: £1.00 for the first book plus 25p per copy for each additional book.

BFPO & EIRE: 55p for the first book, 22p for the second book plus 14p per copy for the next 7 books, thereafter 8p per book.

Sphere Books reserve the right to show new retail prices on covers which may differ from those previously advertised in the text or elsewhere, and to increase postal rates in accordance with the PO.